Why Not Just Be
CHRISTIANS?

Why Not Just Be CHRISTIANS?

VANCE HAVNER

Kingsley Press

Shoals, Indiana

Why Not Just Be Christians?

Published by Kingsley Press
PO Box 973
Shoals, IN 47581
USA

Tel. (800) 971-7985
www.kingsleypress.com
E-mail: sales@kingsleypress.com

ISBN: 978-1-937428-51-8

Contents

Preface

I am making bold to venture forth once again with a collection of sermons. Most of them have been preached in meetings throughout the country, and some have appeared in various religious publications. There may be some repetitions here and there—I have made no effort to eliminate all of them. Some things are worth saying several times; some are not worth saying the first time. I hope that in this case there may be an abundance of the first and not much of the second.

I am thankful for the privilege of preaching for half a century. These messages sum up the major emphases of these years. I have endeavored to avoid riding hobbies and getting off on tangents. I would hope that the title of this volume and the first sermon in it would sound the keynote of the whole book. After all, why not just be Christians?

Vance Havner

Chapter 1

Why Not Just Be Christians?

... the disciples were called Christians first in Antioch (Acts 11:26).

S ome time ago I rode along a modern highway in an up-to-date automobile on a lovely Sunday afternoon. If I could have forgotten newspaper headlines and radio news reports long enough, I might have imagined that I was in that ideal world of peace and plenty which is the poet's dream. But as I rode along I noticed highway signs that read, "Evacuation Route," meaning of course, "In case of atomic attack, this is the way to get out of town." I was rudely awakened to the irony of a world full of scientific wonders, threatening to blow itself to bits with its own gadgets.

I cannot understand how any intelligent human being can swell up with pride in an hour like this. Any thinking man should be red-faced with embarrassment. Scientifically we are in the graduate school; morally and spiritually we are in kindergarten. Civilization is like an ape playing with matches in a room full of dynamite. We talk of "one world," but it is a "wan world," and what some think are the birth pangs of a new era are but the dying gasps of the age.

When Isaiah wrote, "Watchman, what of the night?" (21:11) he had in mind a sentinel on an ancient city watchtower looking for an enemy with crude weapons of primitive warfare. Today we have lonely outposts in Alaska or Greenland where men watch a radar screen, anticipating the possibility of that awful moment when a fanatic may press a button and bury millions of Americans in a furnace of molten steel.

These ramparts we watch are endangered from without and within. So is the bulwark of Christianity. Our greatest enemy is not without but within. The temple of truth will not be damaged half so much by woodpeckers on the outside as by termites on the inside. Any religious group that boasts room for all shades of doctrine is like a man saying, "We have room in our house for termites—all are welcome." If he makes room for termites, he will soon have no house at all.

If the church would only be the church—if Christians would only *be* Christians—nothing could halt our onward march. We are like the early Christians "behind closed doors for fear." We are smitten with an inferiority complex.

The answer is not in church unification. We need not huddle together in self defense; we need to scatter in all directions preaching the Word. We have the answer to our problems and to everybody else's problems. We were here first. The early church faced a pagan civilization, but they did not meet it with panel discussions on Caesar and slavery. Paul did not join a symposium of pagan philosophers to discuss the problems of the times. Whittaker Chambers said, "Communism is no stronger than the failure of other faiths." All of our adversaries are no stronger than the failure of the church to rise to its duty.

How many times have I heard, upon arriving at a church for a meeting, "This will be a poor week for a revival. On Monday night the circus is coming to town; on Tuesday the Sons and Daughters of "I Will Arise" are having a convention; on Thursday night the Garden Club will meet to discuss African violets; the ball game is on Friday night. And there is always television." When was there ever a good week for a revival? Must the church take a back seat in favor of every sideshow that blows into town? Must we take the leftovers? Why shouldn't the other crowd do the worrying? Why shouldn't the church of Jesus Christ—with the answer to all the world's problems—make such an impact that the world, the flesh, and the devil would huddle in consternation, saying, "This will be a poor week for us—there's a revival in town!"

We Christians do not have confidence because there is something wrong with us in both creed and conduct—in what we believe, and in the way we live. We are told that modernism and liberalism are dead, but we are haunted more by their ghosts than we were hurt by their earlier presence. Too many animated question marks are standing in pulpits again, and there are too few living exclamation points. A new theological breeze has begun to blow and a new virus is in the air. The language is different, the personalities are different; the attack is on a new front but the issue is about the same. In the old days the battle was fought in the open, but now it is not fashionable to take a stand against anything. It is a day of diplomats instead of prophets. Defenders of the faith are a weaker breed and are more easily disarmed by the smiling tolerance of the new school of peaceful coexistence. What was black and white has become gray.

In such spiritual fogs and doctrinal twilights, let a minister speak out against heresy and he is declared un-Christian. It has become quite the thing to lambast the fundamentalists, but we are declared lacking in Christian love if we express even a suspicion about wolves in sheep's clothing.

The trumpet is muted and nobody will prepare for battle under such uncertain bugle-blowing. The impression has been created that we preachers cannot speak with authority unless we are Ph.D.'s schooled in existentialism and Bultman. It is hoped that plain grass-roots preachers will not be disturbed by all this avalanche of verbosity. Let Bible believers go right on enjoying the meat of the Word, leaving the bones to the theologians. Some of us are not disturbed about theories of inspiration. We do not believe that the Bible is God's Word only as it applies to you in one verse and to me in another. It is absolute or it is obsolete. It is wired up from heaven and when we make proper contact we get a shock. But if we stay in contact we get a charge! Too many poor souls make only enough contact to get a shock.

The plight of the churches shows up not only in creed but in conduct. The sermon on Sunday is denied by the way most church members live all week. We believe in separation of church and state, but we wish that Christians would become equally concerned about separation of the church and the world. The greatest scandal of Christianity is the low grade of Christian living. There are more professing Christians than ever, but the quality does not keep up with the quantity; we are not improving the sort while we increase the size. We are many but not much. The average church member shows no evidence of having been born again. He is not remotely interested in the deeper Christian life. He is not concerned about forsaking the world, crucifying the flesh, and resisting the devil.

We will not be ready for the challenge of this hour until there is genuine repentance and conversion in our churches, in both creed and conduct. Even earnest and well-meaning Christians tend to divorce doctrine and practice. Some put all the emphasis on orthodoxy, with very little day-by-day living to match. Others major in experience, with little basis in Biblical teaching. One is body without spirit, and the other is spirit without body. Christianity is neither a corpse nor a ghost.

While we are concerned about communism and other "isms"— and we ought to be—why are we so indifferent to an imitation Christianity that so many men speak well of? Not liberalism alone, but dead orthodoxy also, false 'isms" and sects, worldly "churchianity," a form of godliness without power, the miscellaneous mixture of modern Laodiceanism, imposing, popular, prosperous, having need of nothing, lukewarm at a comfortable seventy-two degrees—all of this our Lord will spew from His mouth.

We are not going to meet the challenge of this age by holding *conferences about it*. When doctors have consultations it does not always mean that the condition of the patient is desperate. It may mean that the doctors are desperate. Both patients and doctors are desperate these days, but it will take more than a huddle of ways-and-means committees to meet the situation.

We must be more than *critics of the world situation*. Denunciation of evil has been neglected these days, but it is not enough to expose the unfruitful works of darkness; we must turn the light of a positive Christian testimony upon them. Noah condemned his godless generation, not by lambasting their degeneracy, but by his faith which led him to build an ark to the saving of his household. Too many prophets have warned of coming floods while they failed to get their own families to safety.

On the other hand, we certainly shall not help this age by being *conformists to it.* Getting chummy with Sodom and Gomorrah in order to win them—on the argument that the end justifies the means—will not work. Lot tried that, and lost both his family and his reputation. We are not to be conformed, nor merely non-conformed, but transformed!

The only way to minister effectively to this generation is to be *Christians in it.* I do not mean run-of-the-mill church members, but *Christians* in all the glorious implications of that word. Years ago I saw on a church bulletin board this arresting question: WHY NOT JUST BE CHRISTIANS? I have never forgotten it. It sums up the whole issue. To raise such a question does not discount loyalty to a local church or denomination. The greater loyalty does not exclude the lesser, but rather includes it. One is a better citizen of America if he is first a good citizen in his own town and faithful in his own home. A dog that follows everybody is of no good to anybody. I am not interested in that view of the invisible church which makes a man invisible on Sunday morning in a local church! Charles H. Spurgeon stated it well: "I am not ashamed to be called Calvinist and I do not hesitate to take the name Baptist, but if you ask what my creed is, I say it is Jesus Christ."

A worried airplane passenger asked a calm fellow traveler, "Are you a Christian Scientist?" "No," was the reply, "just a Christian." One never needs to be a Christian plus. It is never Christ *and,* and it is never a Christian *and.* One is Christian or anti-Christian. You do not have to add anything to a Christian, for everything that goes with it is included in that good word.

We Christians do not need unanimity or unification. The only place where you will ever get the saints together is where they are already together, in Jesus Christ. We need more unity of the spirit. There is a common understanding when we are in Him. One does not tune twenty pianos by harmonizing each with the other; they are tuned to a tuning fork, and when each is in tune with the standard pitch, they are in tune with each other. Trying to tune divergent Christian groups to each other is a hopeless business. Only when they are in tune with Christ are they in tune with each other.

The early church faced a pagan civilization with many problems not unlike our own. Those Christians did not sit around discussing current issues in the Roman Empire. They simply dared to be Christians, and they upset the world. The New Testament is not filled with discussions of problems outside the church. Paul and Peter and James and John were occupied with maintaining the purity and power of the church. As long as it had purity and power it took care of itself under God, and empires gave way before it. Today we seek position and popularity and prosperity and that strange thing called "prestige." All of these things avail nothing because we have lost our purity in creed and in conduct, in belief and in practice—and because we have lost our purity, we have lost our power.

Somehow the impression has been created that we need to rethink the inspiration of the Scriptures and revamp all our theology and work out a new code of Christian conduct in line with the times and acceptable to the nuclear age. Actually, this nuclear age is not essentially different from any other age, except for the increase of its gadgets and gimmicks. This is a generation of poor lost sinners and the need of the hour is a fresh crop of New Testament Christians who believe the Bible, trust Christ as Saviour and obey Him as Lord, are filled with the Spirit, and out to make the gospel known.

A lot of time and brains and printers' ink are being wasted these days on the supposition that we must devise some grand new scheme of faith and practice to keep step with missiles and summit conferences and ecumenical get-togethers. Throughout church history God has passed up pompous ecclesiastical assemblages and elaborate programs of experts and has set the world on fire with a handful of all-out Christians who scorn the values of this world and live by rigid discipline, willing to be called "the scum of the earth" and to be made a spectacle to this world for the scandal of the cross.

Why not just be Christians?

CHAPTER 2

Kindling Wood

I am come to send fire on the earth; and what will I, if it be already kindled? (Luke 12:49).

Our Lord came to set the world on fire. It is on fire today, but not with His fire. We have stage fire and strange fire and satanic fire, but not much Spirit-fire. It has been said that the church has become a field for evangelism instead of a force for evangelism. We say that we depend on the Spirit, but actually we are so wired with our own devices that if the fire does not fall from heaven, we can turn on a switch and produce fire of our own; and if there is no sound of a mighty rushing wind, the furnace is set to blow hot air instead. God save us from a synthetic Pentecost!

In the meantime other movements are aflame with a zeal that defies persecution, prison, and death. The fanatical zeal of Communists who lose no opportunity to preach their doctrines, puts us comfortable Christians to shame. Dr. Malik of Lebanon says: "I know the Communist leaders. They are utterly devoted to their cause. That is not true of most Americans I know. Why do you not press the battle to victory with the weapon God gave you to win, the heritage of the Christian faith?" Mohammedanism, Buddhism, communism surge ahead, but we are hearing of "the post-Christian era." The professing church rests in a lukewarm Laodiceanism while our Lord commands us, "Be boiling and repent!"

I do not expect the total membership of our churches to catch on fire. Most of the world is under communism, but not all of these millions are devoted Communists. The world was set on fire for communism by a little band, a dedicated minority who sold out to Karl Marx and the devil. A corresponding Gideon's band could make a similar impact for Jesus Christ. They could meet the *demon*-stration of the powers of darkness with a demonstration of the Holy Spirit.

Marshal Ferdinand Foch is reported to have said: "The battle is won the day before." Gideon's battle was won the day before. He started out with thirty-two thousand men, but God said they were too many. We Christians have gathered an unwieldy multitude and as a consequence we furnish our own greatest interference. We cannot reach the goal for stumbling over our own team. What we have thought was mobilization has turned out to be *mob*-ilization.

Humanly, Gideon may have felt more confident with thirty-two thousand men, but God's ways are not our ways. While there is more carnal security in numbers, the battle of the Lord is not won by statistics. There were statistics aplenty in the Book of Acts, but those numbers were a result and not a goal.

We have majored on "drawing the net." We have failed to sort the fish. When Gideon "sorted the fish," twenty-two thousand cowards were dismissed. A corresponding proportion in our churches come not to the help of the Lord against the mighty. They are afraid to take a stand on unpopular issues. They are present at the bugle blowings and flag wavings but, like the Reubenites in the Song of Deborah, they do not go to the battle. They are sentimental but not sacrificial.

Ninety-seven hundred careless soldiers were removed from Gideon's army. We have never had so many Christian soldiers on all fours as today: compromising in attitude, at the mercy of the enemy, forgetting to watch and pray, and to be sober and vigilant.

Gideon was left with three hundred men who were competent and consecrated. I do not mean, in application, that we should dismiss a similar proportion of our church membership; but we do need to win the battle the day before by marshaling a Master's minority who mean business.

Gideon's army carried torches. If our Lord is to set the world on fire, it must be done through human firebrands who rekindle the flame of God within them, as Paul counseled Timothy. Somewhere I have seen an advertisement that read: "Wanted— wicks to burn out for God; oil and light supplied." There has been too much heat without light and too much light without heat. We need to fuse the two and be, like John the Baptist, burning and shining lights.

Every revival begins with a Gideon's band, a core of effectives, the church within the church. The Revolutionary War had its Minute Men. We need a nucleus of Last-minute Men as the age draws near its close. We are not going to set this world on fire by condemnation of it or by conformity to it, but by the combustion within it of lives ignited by the Holy Spirit.

Any Christian who seeks to find and follow God's program for these days must keep in mind several things. First, there is the promise of our Lord's return. The church missed the road when she stopped looking for the King to come back and started building His Kingdom down here under the delusion that it would be brought in by education, reformation, and legislation under religious auspices. The visible Kingdom will be set up by the King when He returns.

Second, there is the possibility of a great revival. There have been such awakenings in the past and it's about time we had another. Yet, revival does not have all the answers. It has been said that revival is like a sale in a department store: it is spectacular, but the main business is done in the daily merchandising the year around. Pentecost was a great day, but steady growth came as the Lord added daily. Revivals make headlines, but when the records are added up at the last day, it will be found that the main work of the church will have been done in the faithful preaching of ordinary pastors, the day-by-day witnessing of ordinary Christians, the steady soul-winning in Sunday school, in personal evangelism, and in the home.

In the third place, while we look for the Lord to return and while we pray for revival, we can be faithful Christians day by day. Some who spend their time studying prophecy and praying for national revival do very little in the local church and in daily witnessing.

Is this all we can do? No, there is one thing more. We can start a crash program of a *faithful-few-on-fire* in home, church, and community. Let it not be forgotten that Gideon had too many people at the outset. God knew they would claim the credit for the victory. We have too many in the church today—too many of the kind that most of them are! It is almost impossible to get people to pray nowadays, and one reason is evident: the kind of church program many of us are putting over does not require the miraculous presence and power of the Holy Spirit. We can do it ourselves by promotion, enthusiasm, and hard work, so why pray? Then we boast, "Mine own hand hath saved me" (Judges 7:2). A Gideon's band reduced to holy desperation gives God a chance to make the difference—and God gets the glory.

I grew up in the country in a house high on a hill. We had air conditioning in those days! On cold winter mornings I had to build fires. (Dad always went to bed when the rest of us wanted to stay up and got up when we wanted to stay in bed.) I started my fire with kindling wood. I did not try to set the backlog ablaze first. We have been trying to kindle revival fires with a backlog of unconverted and undedicated church members. We need to begin with our kindling wood—men and women and young people who are available, inflammable, expendable. Some may feel that they are too small and weak, but forest fires often begin with only a spark. God can start a big fire with a little kindling wood.

In World War II a handful of British airmen saved London during the blitz. Winston Churchill said, "Never was so much owed by so many to so few." If I may change his words a bit, I would say of God's remnant today—debtors as they are to Greek and barbarian, to wise and unwise—"Never was so much owed by so *few* to so *many!*" God needs not a host, but a handful who will let Him kindle a flame of sacred love in their hearts, and who will pray:

May Thy rich grace impart
Strength to my fainting heart,
My zeal inspire;
As Thou hast died for me,
O may my love to Thee
Pure, warm, and changeless be,
A living fire!

CHAPTER 3

Getting Used to the Dark

And have no fellowship with the unfruitful works of darkness, but rather reprove them (Ephesians 5:11).

Some time ago a friend of mine took me to a restaurant where they must have loved darkness rather than light. I stumbled into the dimly-lit cavern, fumbled for a chair, and mumbled that I needed a flashlight in order to read the menu. When the food came I ate it by faith and not by sight. Gradually, however, I began to make out objects a little more clearly. My host said, "Funny, isn't it, how we get used to the dark?" "Thank you," I replied, "You have given me a new sermon subject."

We are living in the dark. The closing chapter of this age is dominated by the prince and powers of darkness. Men love darkness rather than light because their deeds are evil. The night is far spent; the blackness is more extensive and more excessive as it deepens just before the dawn. Mammoth Cave is not limited to Kentucky; it is universal!

Strangely enough, man never had more artificial illumination and less true light. Bodily, he walks in unprecedented brilliance, while his soul dwells in unmitigated night. He can release a nuclear glory that outdazzles the sun, and with it he plans his own destruction. He can put satellites in the sky, and left to himself, he is a wandering star to whom is reserved the blackness of darkness forever.

The depths of present-day human depravity are too vile for any word in our language to describe. We are seeing not ordinary moral corruption, but evil double-distilled and compounded in weird, uncanny, and demonic combinations and concoctions of iniquity never heard of a generation ago. This putrefaction of the carcass of civilization awaiting the vultures of judgment is not confined to Skid Row; it shows up in the top brackets of society. Plenty of prodigals live morally among swine while garbed in purple and fine linen. A Bishop once said: "There is no difference in reality between the idle rich and the idle poor, between the crowds who loaf in gorgeous hotels and the crowds who tramp the land in rags, save the difference in the cost of their wardrobes and the price of their meals."

Man lives in the dark and even his nuclear flashlight cannot pierce it. We not only live in the dark, we get used to it. There is a slow, subtle, sinister brainwashing process going on and by it we are gradually being desensitized to evil. Little by little, sin is made to appear less sinful until the light within us becomes darkness—and how great is that darkness! Our magazines are loaded with accounts of sordid crime, our newsstands with concentrated corruption. We are engulfed in a tidal wave of pornographic filth. Television has put us in the dark with Sodom and Gomorrah—right in the living room. We get used to it, acclimated to it. We accept, as a matter of course, its art, its literature, its music, its language. We learn to live with it without an inner protest.

Lot was a righteous man, but he moved into Sodom, lived in it, probably became its mayor. His soul was vexed from day to day with the Sodomites' unlawful deeds, but he lost his influence with his family and had to flee for his life. He died in disgrace. I have met many Lots in the past few years! "As it was in the days of Lot ... even thus shall it be in the day when the Son of man is revealed" (Luke 17:28-30). Modern Lots tell us that we should hobnob with Sodom and get chummy with Gomorrah in order to convert them. But the end does not justify the means. Such people do not turn the light on in Sodom—they merely get used to the dark.

The worst of all is that such people get so used to the dark that they think it is growing brighter. Sit long enough in a dark room and you will imagine that more light is breaking in. Men who dwell too long in darkness fancy the day is dawning. We call "broadminded tolerance" what is really peaceful coexistence with evil. It is an effort to establish communion between light and darkness, a concord between Christ and Belial.

This condition extends into the religious world and even into evangelical Christianity. It is possible to fraternize with unbelievers until false doctrine becomes less and less objectionable. We come to terms with it and would incorporate it into the fellowship of truth. We begin by opening doors to borderline sects who "believe almost as we do." Others find overtures from Rome attractive. Still others would make a crazy quilt of world religions, a syncretism of "the best in all faiths." "Syncretism" is only a big word for "hash." These theological chefs who are busy mixing Mulligan stews think the darkness is lifting; the truth is that they are merely getting used to it.

The same danger exists with regard to worldliness. One may live in a twilight zone, in conditions of low visibility, until he finds the practices of this world less repulsive. He mistakes the stretching of his conscience for the broadening of his mind. He renounces what he calls the "Pharisaism" and "puritanism" of earlier days with a good word for dancing, smoking, and even cocktails now and then. Instead of passing up Vanity Fair, he spends his vacations there. John Bunyan tells us that his pilgrims were quite a novelty to the worldlings: "And as they wondered at their apparel, so they did likewise at their speech; for few could understand what they said. They naturally spoke the language of Canaan; but they that kept the Fair were men of this world. So that from one end of the Fair to the other, they seemed barbarians to each other." How out of date that sounds! Operators of Vanity Fair would see little difference in the clothes, conversation, and conduct of most professing Christians today. If the proprietors of that Fair beheld the modern church member, especially in the summertime, wearing in public a garb in which he should never have left the house or even come downstairs, they would not seem barbarians to each other! Bunyan's pilgrims were not getting used to the dark.

Of course we do not get used to it all of a sudden. Alexander Pope described the gradual process:

Vice is a monster of such frightful mien,
As to be hated needs but to be seen;
Yet seen too oft, familiar with her face,
We first endure, then pity, then embrace.

Here is how it works. A secular journal says: "The desensitization of 20th-century man is more than a danger to the common safety.... *There are some things we have no right ever to get used to. One...* is brutality. The other is the irrational. Both... have now come together and are moving towards a dominant pattern." There was a time when sin shocked us. But as the brainwashing progresses, what once amazed us only amuses us. We laugh at the shady joke; tragedy becomes comedy; we learn to speak the language of Vanity Fair.

I heard a preacher tell a doubtful joke to a man of this world. Evidently he wanted to give the impression that preachers are used to the dark; actually he was accommodating himself to the dungeon of this age. Dr. John H. Jowett describes this peril of the preacher: "We are tempted to leave our noontide lights behind in our study and to move among men with a dark lantern which we can manipulate to suit our company. We pay the tribute of smiles to the low business standard. We pay the tribute of laughter to the fashionable jest. We pay the tribute of easy tolerance to ambiguous pleasures. We soften everything to a comfortable acquiescence. We seek to be all things to all men to please all. We run with the hare and hunt with the hounds. We become the victims of illicit compromise. There is nothing distinctive about our character." That applies to more people than preachers!

The housewife who moves into suburbia and wants to go along with the group spirit of the community faces the same temptation. So does the organization man at the boss's party or the student on a pagan campus. There are new techniques for socializing at Vanity Fair, but Bunyan's pilgrims had the right idea. We are not here to learn how to live in the dark but to walk in the light. We are not here to get along with evil but to overcome it with good.

One of the signs of getting used to the dark is the way we excuse sin. We give it new names: adultery is free love; the drunkard is an alcoholic; sodomy is homosexuality; the murderer is temporarily insane. Church workers fall into grievous sin and move on to new positions without repentance or change of conduct. Parents let down in discipline, saying, "What's the use?" Pastors give up preaching against sin, arguing that the world's evils are here to stay and since church members are not going to be any better we might as well accept the status quo and live with it. We see this mixture of light and darkness in television programs that join worldliness with hymns. We see it in Hollywood portraying the Bible.

The world lives in the dark because it rejects Jesus Christ, the Light of the world: "And this is the condemnation, that light is come into the world, and men loved darkness rather than light, because their deeds were evil" (John 3:19). The word here translated "condemnation" is "crisis" in the original. The coming of Christ precipitated a crisis. It compels men in the very nature of things to come to the light or abide in darkness. This light shines in the Saviour: "I am the light of the world..." (John 8:12). It shines in the Scriptures: "Thy word is a lamp unto my feet, and a light unto my path" (Psalm 119:105). It shines in the saints: "Ye are the light of the world" (Matthew 5:14). "Every one that doeth evil hateth the light, neither cometh to the light, lest his deeds should be reproved" (John 3:20). That explains why some people do not come to church.

I remember a couple in my first pastorate. The husband, an unsaved man, brought his wife to church on Sunday nights, but he sat outside in his car. He was in the dark in more ways than one because he did not like to face the gospel light. His wife enjoyed the service because she loved the light and came to the light that her deeds might be made manifest that they were wrought in God. When you overturn a stone in the field and the sunlight strikes beneath it, all the hidden creeping and crawling things scurry for cover. So do our sinful hearts grow restless under the light of God's truth. In an unlighted cellar you do not see the spiders and snakes and lizards and toads until the light breaks in. So men do not realize their sinfulness until they face the Light. No wonder some live in the dark all week and then blink their eyes and wince in church on Sunday morning when the preacher turns on the Light! They have photophobia—they fear the Light.

Our business as Christians is to let our light shine: "... have no fellowship with the unfruitful works of darkness, but rather reprove [expose, turn the light on] them" (Ephesians 5:11). We expose them not so much by denunciation, although that has its place, but by the contrast of our godly living. Alas, we are so afraid of being offensive that we are not effective! Our Lord said that two things would smother the light of our testimony, a bushel and a bed. Today we dim our light in a third way: we turn it low for fear of creating a disturbance; we shade it to match the dim dungeon of this age. We would rather grieve the Holy Spirit than offend the wicked.

The early Christians did not dim their lights to match the times. Paul exceedingly troubled the places he visited, and even in prison at midnight he turned night into day. The saints in Rome lighted the streets with their burning bodies. Christians met in catacombs, but they illuminated the world.

We are a city set on a hill, not hidden in a dungeon. We are to shine as lights in the world. This is no time to get used to the dark; it is time to turn on the Light! Too long have the caverns of this world been undisturbed. Of course some cave dwellers will squirm, but others will see our good works and glorify our Father in heaven. Light has no communion with darkness. We are not here to commune with it but to conquer it, and "this is the victory that overcometh the world, even our faith" (1 John 5:4).

Early Christianity set the world aglow because absolute Light was pitched against absolute darkness. The early Christians believed that the gospel was the only hope of the world, that without it all men were lost and all religions false. The day came when the church and the world mixed light and darkness. The church got used to the dark and lived in it for several centuries, with only occasional flashes of light. Today too many Christians think there is some darkness in our light and some light in the world's darkness. We half-doubt our own gospel and half-believe the religion of this age. We are creeping around in the dark when we should be flooding the world with light. We need to get our candles out from under bushels and beds, take off the shades of compromise and let them shine in our hearts, our homes, our businesses, our churches, and our communities with that light that shines in the Saviour and in the Scriptures and in the saints.

Chapter 4

"Something Wrong With the Mixture"

... the fire shall try every man's work of what sort it is (1 Corinthians 3:13).

Years ago I heard a minister tell a story about two boys at the scene of an earthquake. One of them picked up some mortar from a fragile building that had collapsed, crumbled it in his hands, and said, "Something's wrong with the mixture." The material was not equal to the emergency.

That something is wrong with the mixture is evident today in the things we buy. One would think, judging by the advertisements, that our products would be the best ever produced—every item of highest grade in material, construction, and performance. But if you have stocked up on modern machines, gadgets, and appliances, you know better. They are not made of stuff that will stand wear and tear. They are made to wear out quickly so that "the waste-makers," as we consumers have been called, will buy the next model. "Top Prices for Junk" could be hung over more things than commonly go by that name.

Something is wrong with the mixture, not only in what we buy, but in what we build. I used to admire the solid structure of the old First Baptist Church of Charleston, South Carolina, where I was pastor. Those foundations and pillars and walls were built to endure. When Archibald Rutledge rebuilt his ancestral home near Charleston, he discovered that "the hand-hewn sleepers and beams were as firm and solid as they were two hundred years ago." There was nothing wrong with the mixture in those days.

Once I was riding with some friends just outside Washington. As we crossed a bridge someone said, "Funny thing about this bridge. When they started to build a new one, they found that the old foundations were better than any they can build now, so they built a new bridge on the old foundations." I wish we would do more of that kind of building!

When one looks at the original copies of the Declaration of Independence and the Constitution of the United States, he is convinced that those historic documents were put together well. Those men took time to write a masterpiece. We haven't turned out anything like that lately! Newton D. Baker wondered whether they could have produced what they did if they had been under the blinding glare of modern publicity. Abe Lincoln wrote his Gettysburg speech himself, and it took only six minutes to deliver it, but it endures. He was not on radio, where one has to keep talking whether he says anything or not. He lived before the age of ghostwriters (the Phantom Era). No wonder there is no body to so many speeches now! There was nothing wrong with the mixture in those days.

The "cheap stuff" shows up in character. We live in a gigantic build-up of sham and pretense, veneer and tinsel and ballyhoo, a shoddy Tower of Babel, a colossal fraud, a rickety creation of wood, hay, and stubble, a superficial wonderland of freaks, sleight-of-hand, hocus-pocus, and Hollywood. We are not turning out character that can stand life's wear and tear. It shows up in divorce rates because men and women lack the integrity to keep the marriage contract. It is revealed in crime waves and juvenile delinquency. A wealthy father sent his son to a fashionable school, and when the boy was expelled later, the irate father wrote to the principal: "I sent my boy there for you to make a man out of him." The principal replied, "When you don't send us anything to start with, we can't send you anything back."

We cannot even entertain ourselves. We have to pay professionals to do it. A prominent psychologist said, "Americans are constantly running away from themselves. We bore ourselves. We have not learned to contemplate. We hardly ever take time to walk, to be alone, to think and reflect." Thousands cannot sleep without artificial aid. Suicides, insanity, nervous breakdowns—it all adds up to this: there is something wrong with the mixture.

The international situation declares it. Because of this fundamental weakness the League of Nations failed, and our modern glass house in Manhattan is only another monument to the same trouble. Will Rogers said, at the time of the earlier Disarmament Conferences, "Those fellows might get somewhere if it wasn't for human nature." The Chinese have a proverb: "You cannot carve rotten wood." We cannot create an enduring human brotherhood because the material is faulty.

In keeping with the times we have a cheap Christianity that does not cost us much. The shame and reproach of the old rugged cross means nothing more than a line in a hymnbook to the average church member. We sing, "Am I a soldier of the Cross?"—but if Uncle Sam's soldiers went about their business as do most of the Lord's army, they would end up in the guardhouse. There is something wrong with the mixture in most Christians today. Paul used athletic terms to describe Christian experience; now the athletes of this world discipline themselves to win corruptible crowns. When one considers the sloppy living of so many professing Christians who claim to be running the greatest of races, fighting the greatest of battles, working for an eternal prize, he can only hang his head in shame.

Christianity is not a happiness cult; it is not a success cult. At heart it is the process by which God makes saints out of sinners. We are predestinated to be conformed to the image of God's Son. We are not on a glorified picnic, a sanctified hayride. We are afflicted nowadays with a cheap Christianity, a kind of religious popcorn diet—no cross, no discipline! We receive the Word with joy, but we have no root nor depth and are soon offended. There are too many religious hoboes trying to go to heaven as cheaply as possible, with just enough prayer, Bible reading, and service to get by. Such lives will go up in smoke at the judgment. Paul tells us that the only sure foundation is Jesus Christ and that we should build on that foundation with gold, silver, and precious stones if our lives are to stand the fire test. Alas, we mix wood, hay, and stubble, and there is something wrong with the mixture!

Paul also tells us: "But with me it is a very small thing that I should be judged of you, or of man's judgment: yea, I judge not mine own self" (1 Corinthians 4:3). "Man's judgment" here means "man's day," and what a pitiful little day it is! I can imagine some of Paul's contemporaries saying, "Too bad about Saul of Tarsus. He had a good start, was a brilliant student under Gamaliel. Then he had something like a sunstroke and has been a religious fanatic ever since. He gets into jail every once in a while—What a tragedy!" But we are still reading Paul while his contemporaries are forgotten. They measured by man's little day; he lived in the light of eternity. He had his eye on *that day* and His Master's "well done." Today the big idea is just to get the job done and collect the pay. We are not interested in the well-done job. I read recently of a man who was expelled from an organization for doing his work too well! A business executive said, "This country is experiencing the great era of the goof-off, the age of the half-done job.... The land from coast to coast has been enjoying a stampede away from responsibility."

This generation wants privilege without responsibility, the crown without the cross, the sweet without the bitter, the delights without the duties. We want the advantages of America without shouldering the responsibilities of being Americans. We want the privileges of marriage while we dodge the responsibilities of the home. Young people want the benefits of home without obeying their parents. Everybody joins church but a corporal's guard does the work and pays the bills. If churches had to depend on three-fourths of their membership, they couldn't operate. Christians "accept" Christ as Saviour but refuse to obey Him as Lord. Yes, we are enjoying a stampede away from responsibility. No wonder something is wrong with the mixture!

It costs to build with gold, silver, and precious stones, so we use wood, hay, and stubble. We may get by now, but the day will declare it, the fire test will reveal it. We shall be happy then if we have built wisely and well. When we view the edifice of a fireproof life, we may ask, "Lord, where did that gold rafter come from?" and He will answer, "That is when the devil told you to go to bed, but you prayed on to victory." "Where did I get that silver beam?" "That is when you were reconciled to your offended brother." "Where did those rubies and sapphires come from?" "Those are the souls you won to Christ." It costs, but it pays! Only this is success.

Babe Ruth once told of a humble preacher he had known, a godly man indeed. Babe said, "I've signed my name on hundreds of baseballs. He wrote his on human hearts. I am called a great homerunner but, compared to him, I didn't make first base."

Are you on the foundation of Christ Jesus? How are you building? Beware lest the Great Day shall reveal something wrong with the mixture. It costs to build with fireproof material—but it pays!

CHAPTER 5

Sounding a New Testament "A"

*For if the trumpet give an uncertain sound, who shall prepare himself
to the battle? (1 Corinthians 14:8).*

If wringing our hands over the times and bemoaning the religious situation today could do it, the millennium would be
here by now. Almost every other article in our church papers and
every other book in our religious bookstores dwells on the same
sad theme: "Are we living in the post-Christian era?" Church
activity at a record high, national morals at a record low; the
slump in ministerial candidates and missionary volunteers—on
and on it goes, and if you have read one, you have read all. It is
about time we declared a moratorium. We know what the trouble is and we know the answer, but we are afraid to do anything
about it.

Our business today is to be New Testament Christians, proclaim New Testament Christianity, and build New Testament
churches. That sounds simple enough, commonplace in fact, but
just try it in dead-earnest and see what happens! Immediately a
mighty howl will go up from worldly church members, the mixed
multitude that prefer Egypt's garlic to Canaan's glory; from status seekers who joined the church because it helps business, and
who will write out a check now and then but would never dream
of putting themselves on God's collection plate; from all who
profess Christ as Saviour but reject Him as Lord. They all say the
same thing: "There is no perfect church."

We are not talking about a perfect church; we are talking about
a New Testament church. The New Testament churches were not
perfect but they had a standard—and it was not imperfection!
They sought to live up to that standard, and dealt with anybody

who tried to lower it. Today the New Testament flag is far ahead of the regiment. There are those who would bring it back to the doctrine and experience of the average church member. We need rather to bring the regiment up to the flag!

A couple had danced till morning in the fetid air of a night-club. As they walked out on the street one asked the other, "What is that I smell?" "That's fresh air!" was the reply. The fresh air of normal New Testament Christianity would be a shock to the average professing Christian. The standard of living among most of our church people is so low that one would have to backslide to be in fellowship with them!

We have standard time and we set our watches by it. What pandemonium if everyone kept his own kind of time! We have standard pitch in music and we tune our instruments by it. Suppose every member of the choir insisted on a different pitch? (I've heard some choirs that came dangerously near that!) We need to tune in to New Testament pitch, and if we ever do, we shall discover how flat we are! We must accept the New Testament standard, affirm it, and act upon it. To insist on being New Testament Christians, preaching New Testament Christianity, and building New Testament churches means that we would stop passing resolutions and begin promoting revolutions of the Acts-of-the-Apostles kind. Of course that creates a commotion. A dear brother at prayer meeting prayed, "Lord, if there should be a spark of fire in this meeting, please water that spark!"

Too many dear souls are afraid of a heavenly disturbance. The gospel makes some people sad, some mad, and some glad. It is better that people should go out of church mad than merely to go out, neither sad, mad, nor glad. We are going to have to pay the price of self-denying discipleship and start all over again, or else God will have to begin anew with some humble crowd on the other side of the railroad tracks.

Most religious movements begin in a cave and end in a cathedral. David began in the cave of Adullam, with a handful of men who were out to make him a king. It's about time we recruited another David's band, in another cave of Adullam, whose only business is to make David's Son the King of kings and Lord of lords in their lives.

Dr. A. J. Gordon transformed a cold Boston congregation into a flaming New Testament church. He did not do it by starting a new church down the street, nor by excommunicating the unfaithful, but by developing a "church within the church." He was a New Testament Christian; he preached New Testament Christianity and he built a New Testament church. Today we are a long way from the original. "This" is not "that!" I have heard of a man who boasted that he possessed an axe that dated back to George Washington's time. "Of course," he admitted, "it has worn out two heads and five handles!" Much of modern Christianity is just about that original!

Dr. Gordon said, "A few Spirit-filled disciples are sufficient to save a church. The Holy Ghost acting through these can and does bring back recovery and health to the whole church."

Can the fire be rekindled in an old church? Yes, if the church will pay the price. Dr. R. A. Torrey used to say that it begins when a few members get thoroughly right with God. It begins with a dedicated minority who, after confession and cleansing and commitment, have been filled with the Spirit. When that fire breaks out, worldly and indifferent church members will complain, and one of two things will happen: the undedicated majority will smother the fire of the Gideon's band; or the flaming few will set the other crowd on fire (at least they can make it so hot that some may go to another church where they can sleep on Sunday morning in a service geared to give them what they want instead of what they need).

The top item on our agenda today is to get back to the beginning. We never become so literary that we do not need the alphabet. We never become such music masters that we get away from the scale. It is possible to become so involved in spiritual mathematics that we forget simple arithmetic. Dr. J. B. Gambrell was exercised over this tendency years ago. He wrote: "Not since the beginning of the Christian era has anyone heard so much about the business end of religion, nor so much good figuring

on how long it will take to convert the world, nor such nice cal-
culations on how many dollars it takes to convert a soul. We are
in a day of planning and of figuring. Certain men have gotten
themselves before the world as great religious statesmen. We are
almost dazed with the magnificence of some of their conceptions, and their methods are so fine that the common man feels
that he does not know where to begin.... Getting away from the
tumult and reading the New Testament quietly and thinking it
over, I am writing it down now deliberately, that all this 'looking
over' the situation, 'considering the circumstances' and 'figuring'
on the millennium and parceling out the world to be converted in a given time, and fitting up a nice harness for everybody
to work in, makes me tired. While the experts are telling us all
about it and organizing everything, some men that don't seem to
know much are holding great meetings and nearly all the people
that are converted at all now are converted by non-experts....
Before we know it we are going to be snared by human wisdom
and human devices. We will get away from the simple method
of Christ which is so simple that any people can understand it....
After a while we will wake up and find that we have been weav-
ing some very fine theories that will enslave us and play us out."

That was written years ago, and we *are* nearly "played out,"
plunging here and there in these frantic times. We waste ourselves on futile projects not in God's program. It is time to follow
the Bible pattern and begin a new fellowship—the true church
within the professing church. Like Israel of old, the church bows
today before the golden calf of this age. We need a Moses to call
God's people back to the place of separation and obedience. As
when the Saviour healed the blind man, the modern synagogue
may exclude men and women who have had a real experience
of Christ; but outside the synagogue, today as then, such men
and women will meet their Lord and establish a new center of
worship. The writer to the Hebrews bids us go to the Saviour
outside the camp bearing His reproach. The old rugged cross still
stands outside the city walls of most organized religion today. In
the closing chapter of this age we need to gather a company, the

assembly of the "anyones," who will hear His voice and open the door and let Him come in as Guest to abide as Host. These are the true *ecclesia*. The rich, prosperous, lukewarm world-church He will spew from His mouth.

Let every minister face this threefold question for himself: Am I a New Testament Christian? Am I preaching New Testament Christianity? Am I building a New Testament church? Simple questions, but, squarely faced, they could start a one-man revolution. Yet let us not be impatient with imperfection, expecting all church members to become saints overnight. The New Testament churches were a mixture of babes and mature Christians and all stages of growth between. Today, many on our rolls are unsaved and need to be born again. Babes must be fed, worldlings must be brought to repentance, the indifferent must be aroused, the troubled comforted, the faithful encouraged. Some who should be in the advanced school of Christ are still in kindergarten; some are subnormal and some abnormal. There is no perfect church, but there is a world of difference between the preacher and church who hold true to the New Testament ideal and those who accept things as they are as normal and sink to that level. Let us never forget that His church is a sheepfold, not a zoo, and pastors are undershepherds, not keepers of a menagerie.

There is no point in spending our time sighing for *the church that was.* Neither should we settle down in *the church that is,* satisfied with the status quo. We should make our goal *the church that ought to be,* even though we disturb all who rest at ease in Zion. We shall not attain it completely down here, but we can work toward it until that day when we join the church triumphant, *the church that shall be,* a glorious church not having spot or wrinkle or any such thing.

I have heard of a violinist who played each week on a nationwide broadcast. One day he received a letter from an old mountaineer who lived way back of beyond. The letter read, "I've got an old fiddle. It's out of tune and I don't have anything to tune it to. Next time you play, would you mind sounding me a good strong 'A'?" The letter appealed to the musician, and at his next broadcast, before he played, he made this announcement: "Old Timer, I got your letter. Get your old fiddle out. Before I start my program I am going to sound for you a good strong 'A'."

In this bewildered world today, do we not need above all else the sounding of a good strong New Testament "A"?

CHAPTER 6

The Christ of the Emmaus Road

Abide with us, for it is toward evening, and the day is far spent (Luke 24:29).

Jesus had been crucified and buried, and now, three days later, two lonely disciples were trudging home to Emmaus, seven miles out of Jerusalem. They should have been singing, but instead they were sad. They had a heartache instead of a hallelujah. What was meant to be the ground of their hope had become the cause of their doubt, and what should have been a reason for delight had become their despair. They said, "Today is the third day," and because it was, they should have been hilarious. Both the written Word and the living Word had said He would rise on that day. But they were half-believing and half-doubting: "We trusted that it had been he which should have redeemed Israel..."—there was their faith; "... to day is the third day since these things were done" (Luke 24:21)—there lay their doubt.

They were right in their facts but wrong in their conclusion. It was the third day, and exactly because it was, they should not have been sad. The woman at Jacob's well was right in her facts: "Thou hast nothing to draw with, and the well is deep...," but wrong in her conclusion: "... whence then hast thou that living water?" (John 4:11). These disciples had their chronology right and their theology right, but they had no doxology!

All over America I meet modern disciples of the Emmaus Road. Some admit their condition; they come forward in meetings with wet eyes or write letters full of doubt and despondency. Others are too proud or afraid to admit the truth that they are disappointed, not in the Lord, but in their experience of Him. "They trusted," like the Emmaus disciples, but delight has become despair. They wouldn't have anyone in the world know that their experience is not real, so they keep going through the motions of religious activity in a form without force. They say the words and sing the songs, but they are like fountains in public squares where water gushes out of lips that never taste it. These disciples would be awfully embarrassed, after all these years, to confess that they are Emmaus Christians. Yet, when they are alone with their souls and absolutely honest, they know that they live in the bitterness of Romans 7, not in the blessedness of Romans 8. It is not that they don't believe the doctrines; a fundamentalist can be as dry as a modernist. Some are not burdened any more about it. They are resigned to live at a poor dying rate, their love so faint, so cold to Christ, and His love for them so great. At least the Emmaus disciples were troubled over the situation!

Some of the Emmaus disciples are ministers. Some are just out of school, half-believing, half-doubting, having been taught to doubt the Bible instead of believing it. Others are older and have grown disillusioned, disappointed in men they once trusted, cynical over the inconsistencies and hypocrisies of church life. They started out with starry eyes but their golden dreams have lost their glow in the rat-race of religious politics. Too many have tended the vineyards of others to the neglect of their own; they work harder than ever trying to pump water out of a dry well. My heart goes out to them. They do not want to be this way. I do not believe a man would enter the ministry at all unless he had some sort of heavenly vision. But there are more ministers than we realize who secretly hunger for a deeper experience of Jesus Christ, and whose jaded spirits need quickening because they have left their first love and lost the joy of their salvation. Some of them show up in strange meetings and sample queer doctrines and fall in with odd sects, all in desperation, like a drowning man clutching at a straw.

I am convinced that our greatest trouble is not false doctrine or worldliness but an inadequate experience of Jesus Christ. A handful of men and women who loved Jesus and were filled with the Spirit shook the world one time. It could be done again, but never by Emmaus disciples like those who were living on the memory of a dead Christ instead of in communion with the living Lord. And yet, within an hour or two, the same disciples became radiant witnesses. It was said of Thomas Chalmers that he had "an original experience of Jesus Christ." It was his own, not somebody else's. Some of us live on a mosaic of other people's experiences, getting our spiritual thrills by proxy. We read of John Wesley's heartwarming and Hudson Taylor's crisis and Dwight L. Moody's enduement, but if we get no further, these men become not our inspiration but our despair.

The living Christ walks beside us, ready to change us from weaklings to witnesses, to give us the garment of praise for the spirit of heaviness. He may not meet us in a blinding vision or in thrilling ecstasy, but if we have trusted him, and yet our faith has grown dim and dry and disappointing, we have a right to a brand-new experience of the living Christ which will turn us around on the Emmaus Road, straighten our drooping shoulders, and start us out in another direction to bless others even as we have been blessed.

> Lord Jesus, make thyself to me
> A living, bright reality,
> More pleasant to faith's vision keen
> Than any outward object seen;
> More dear, more intimately nigh
> Than e'en the sweetest earthly tie.

When it comes to a deeper experience of Christ, too many only *deplore* the lack of it; some *discuss* theories about it, a few *describe* how to have it, but too few *demonstrate* it. Actually, however, we should not talk so much about "it." Too many are seeking "it" and when they find "it" they think they have arrived. What we need is not merely "it," an experience, but "Him." Some make much of experiences of the Holy Spirit, but F. B. Meyer said long ago that we should beware of making the Holy Spirit the figurehead of any movement. The Holy Spirit testifies of our Lord, not of Himself. The Spirit was *not yet* given because Jesus was *not yet* glorified (John 7:39). That speaks of Pentecost, of course, but it is also true that the Holy Spirit never comes in blessing until Jesus is glorified, whether in individual blessing or in church revival. We would do well to study these two *not yets*.

The Emmaus experience had four characteristics that mark every genuine meeting with the Lord. First, *it was true to the Scriptures*. The risen Lord reproved those disciples for being slow of heart to believe the prophets, and "beginning at Moses and all the prophets, he expounded unto them in all the scriptures the things concerning himself" (Luke 24:27). Not only does the Spirit testify of our Lord, but so do the Scriptures. Our Lord opened the Scriptures, opened the disciples' eyes, and opened their understanding—and He began by opening the Scriptures. We err because we know not the Scriptures. Our eyes are holden if we do not search the Scriptures that testify of Him. Better to be slow of head to understand than slow of heart to believe! The Scriptures are like a railroad track; some dear souls are like a locomotive off the track, stuck in the mud, with only the whistle blowing.

Let it be noted that our Lord began with Moses. If men will not believe Moses and the prophets, neither will they be persuaded though One rose from the dead. Men who doubt or deny the inspiration of the Old Testament part company with Jesus Christ. A genuine experience of Him begins with an open Bible: "Faith cometh by hearing, and hearing by the word of God" (Romans 10:17). I do not agree with those who think we should not begin with the Bible but should relate our experience when dealing with an unsaved man. Philip began at an Old Testament verse and preached Jesus to the Ethiopian eunuch. Our Lord defeated the devil with three verses from Deuteronomy. Our weapon is the Word of God.

The living Word manifests Himself in line with the written Word. Any spiritual experience that is not Bible-based is not of God but of the devil. It may be spiritual, but it is the wrong spirit!

In the second place, the experience of the Emmaus disciples *stirred their hearts.* They said one to another, "Did not our heart burn within us, while he talked with us by the way, and while he opened to us the Scriptures?" (Luke 24:32). He gave them holy heartburn. A genuine experience of the Lord is based on Scripture, not our feelings, but that does not mean that our feelings are unaffected. We are so afraid of feeling these days that it has become almost the unpardonable sin to say "Amen" at prayer meeting. We are not saved because we feel saved, but being saved ought to make us happy. There never was a real revival that did not produce heartburn and hallelujahs. For some years now we have been having "revivals" specially designed not to arouse anybody, and they are certainly working out as planned. Plenty of church members are shaky about what they believe, while not many are shaken by what they believe. The church militant has become the church complacent. We are so afraid of too much feeling that we are almost past feeling. Afraid of too much, we make out with too little. Dead men do not sing or cry; one has to be alive to have feeling, which is true of churches as well. We have moved from burning hearts to itching ears.

John Wesley set England on fire after his heart was strangely warmed. In that drab period between the death of the Puritans and the birth of the Methodists it was an Emmaus heartburn that changed the course of history.

> Thy soul must overflow if thou
> Another's soul wouldst reach;
> It takes the overflow of heart
> To give the lips full speech.

Furthermore, the Emmaus experience *showed up at home.* "Abide with us," the weary disciples besought their Lord, "for it is toward evening, and the day is far spent" (Luke 24:29). It is toward evening in the lives of many of us; it is toward the end of the age with all of us. It is later than we think. The time is short and we need to pray:

Abide with me from morn till eve,
For without Thee I cannot live;
Abide with me when night is nigh,
For without Thee I cannot die.

Never was the old hymn more timely:

Swift to its close ebbs out life's little day;
Earth's joys grown dim, its glories pass away;
Change and decay in all around I see;
O Thou, who changest not, abide with me."

It is not enough to see the Lord in the Scriptures. It is not enough that He stirs our hearts. Feelings will rise and fall, and zeal will flag. We need His abiding presence all the time. Mind you, He did not manifest Himself at Emmaus in a great sermon or a dazzling performance, but in the breaking of bread, the simplest and plainest of things. That was not a miraculous meal like the feeding of the multitude, nor a special meal like the Lord's Supper. It was a common household meal, and yet it was miraculous and special because His presence made it so.

If ever our homes needed the Lord, it is now. The domestic life of America is one vast disaster area. Our homes have gone to pieces, and unless Christ gets into more of them we face worse evils here than any abroad.

Christians need a fresh revelation of the Lord in their homes. Too often we lay aside our Christian profession with our Sunday clothes, behaving worst before those who love us most. He is a poor saint who smiles at everybody else's table and sits at his own like such a son of Belial that one cannot speak to him. Some have Sunday-morning grace and Bible-conference grace, but no kitchen or living-room grace. If the Saviour cannot manifest Himself at your breakfast table He will not shine through you at any other table. If it takes two cups of coffee to make you fit to live with of a morning, you need the Emmaus experience.

Finally, this experience of the lonely disciples *sent them out to witness:* "They told what things were done in the way..." (Luke 24:35). They did not sit with folded hands and congratulate each other. It was a day of good tidings and they did not hold their peace. One thinks of the spiritual with the constant refrain, "I couldn't keep it to myself." The disciples hurried back to Jerusalem to tell others, and as they witnessed, the Lord appeared again! He said to them, "Ye are witnesses of these things" (Luke 24:48).

We are awfully short on the kind of Christian experience that makes us tell about Him. Some want to be His lawyers, arguing His case, but while He sometimes needs apologists, He needs apostles more. We do not have a secret to be hidden but a story to be heralded. Sometimes it is easier to give a check for the telling of the story in Africa than to tell it around the corner. A fresh experience of the Lord gives witnessing its dynamic. Some have the desire and know the directions, but they don't do it because they lack dynamic. When the Lord takes over He cures us of believing the heresy that only a few special people are missionaries.

How does one come into the Emmaus experience? What did those disciples do? For one thing, they were concerned. At least they were discussing it; it was on their minds and lay heavy on their hearts. Too many of us do not care. Then they constrained Him when "he made as though he would have gone further" (Luke 24:28). Our Lord does not force Himself upon us—He will go on if we do not constrain Him—yet He longs to abide with us. Have you not, in the company of someone you loved, moved as though you would be going, yet inwardly you hoped you would be asked to remain? He is *the Guest who would go on.* The deeper things of God pass on if we do not lay hold upon them. But He is also *the Guest who will come in:* "Behold, I stand at the door, and knock: if any man hear my voice, and open the door, I will come in..." (Revelation 3:20). Moreover, He is *the Guest who becomes the Host:* "I... will sup with him, and he with me" (Revelation 3:20). He comes in as the Guest; He abides as the Host. It was that way at Cana and Emmaus. It will be so with you.

For most of us the top item on the agenda of life is a new experience of the living Christ, one that is true to the Scriptures, stirs our hearts, shows up at home, and sends us forth to witness until, in the glow of that testimony, He appears again!

CHAPTER 7

The Menace of Moderatism

Be not righteous over much; neither make thyself over wise: why shouldest thou destroy thyself? Be not over much wicked, neither be thou foolish: why shouldest thou die before thy time? (Ecclesiastes 7:16, 17).

The greatest peril we face today is not extremism, serious as that is, but moderatism. By "moderatism" I do not mean "moderation." The Scriptures teach moderation—temperance that avoids excess—but moderatism is something else. The writer of Ecclesiastes says: "Be not righteous over much; neither make thyself over wise: why shouldest thou destroy thyself? Be not over much wicked, neither be thou foolish: why shouldest thou die before thy time?" (7:16-17). Bible scholars have differed as to the interpretation of this passage. It could well be the creed of the middle-of-the-roader: "Be moderately religious and moderately wicked."

The middle of the road is a poor place to walk. It is a poor place to drive. It is a poor place to live. Moderatism stands with the multitude at Carmel while Elijah cries, "How long halt ye between two opinions?" and answers him "not a word" (1 Kings 18:21). The moderatist cannot understand our Lord's saying, "I would thou wert cold or hot" (Revelation 3:15). "Is it not better to be lukewarm than cold?" the moderatist argues. "Is it not better to go half-way than never to start?"

The moderatist works both sides of the street. He may sip wine at the Lord's table on Sunday morning and take his cocktail on Sunday night. He makes sacred things common and dignifies the profane. He slaps God on the back in cheap familiarity with "the Big Buddy Upstairs." He is the product of this age of world conformity, of peaceful coexistence with sin, that glorifies the great general average. He pulls down the high and builds up the low to one common level.

It is the moderate drinker who keeps up the whiskey business. It is the moderate drinker who causes most of the automobile accidents. The all-out drunk is thrown into the back seat while the moderatist sits at the wheel with multiplied horsepower at his hand but no horse sense in his head. It is the church-office-holding moderate drinker who is a bigger asset to the devil than all the bums in the back alleys. He is one reason why sermons that used to call for total abstinence have now been softened to appeals for "temperance." A magazine asked, "Are American Women Drinking Too Much?" If they are drinking at all, they are drinking too much!

Such moderatism raises no protest when tobacco is advertised, not by lung-cancer victims, but by attractive girl smokers; when dancing is made respectable by church sanction; when Hollywood, that cesspool of moral corruption, portrays the Bible and the clergy give it approval. Moderatism smudges black and white into indefinite gray. Its theology is fundamentalist-modern and modernist-fundamental. The Lord's sheep are painted gray instead of white, and thereby all black sheep are less conspicuous.

In World War I Theodore Roosevelt blasted German-Americans who had divided loyalties. He called them "hyphenated Americans" and said, "America is not a polyglot boarding house." Moderatists would make the church a polyglot boarding house, filled with hyphenated Christians. Roosevelt said, "If a man is an American and something else, he is not an American." That could be said of a Christian. Billy Sunday used to say of worldly Christians, "You might as well talk about a heavenly devil." James tells us that the friend of the world is the enemy of God. Our Lord said, "He that is not with me is against me; and he that gathereth not with me scattereth abroad" (Matthew 12:30). A man who is faithful to his wife part of the time is not faithful at all. A man who is partly faithful to his family or his country or his church is a traitor. A divided loyalty is not loyalty at all. With Jesus Christ it is "all or nothing." Moderatism would split devotion and be both moderately righteous and moderately evil.

The moderatist makes much of tolerance. He mistakes the stretching of his conscience for the broadening of his mind. The Word of God says, "Ye that love the Lord, hate evil..." (Psalm 97:10). We Christians are to abstain from all appearance of evil and to abhor it, not tolerate it. Some things cannot be tolerated. Sin is moral leprosy, and to put up with leprosy is to die with it. Sin is spiritual cancer, and the man who tries to live with it dies of it. If we do not deal with malignancy it will deal with us, and malignancy tolerates nothing. The Israelites tolerated the Canaanites instead of exterminating them, and they were overcome by them. The church in Thyatira had love, *agape,* love in its highest form; but it also tolerated Jezebel and the Lord dealt with it in judgment. We tolerate false doctrine and worldliness under the guise of Christian charity. But such words as "abhor," "abstain," and "hate" leave no room for being chummy with evil.

There is such a thing as extremism, and true moderation avoids extremes. But a true New Testament Christian would be called an extremist today. They were so called in the early church. Our Lord was accused of being beside Himself, and so was Paul. True moderation is what the moderatist calls "extreme." We are so subnormal that we call the normal "abnormal"!

The outstanding moderatist of the New Testament was Gamaliel. When the apostles were on trial he took to the middle of the road. I once thought that his speech was sober and level-headed. Actually he was an appeaser who turned the meeting into a Munich. He was a Chamberlain without an umbrella. He was the apostle of compromise, neither for nor against. He made a false comparison, suggested a false criterion, and arrived at a false conclusion. Paul started out as an opposer and ended as an apostle; he was never an appeaser. You could always tell which side of the fence he was on. He never sat on the fence with Gamaliel who was more interested in keeping things quiet in Jerusalem than in standing with Jesus Christ.

The great moderatist of Luther's day was Erasmus. It was said that he could shade down "yes" until it sounded like "no" and burnish up "no" until it almost passed for "yes." He lived as though our Lord had said, "Let your yea be nay and your nay yea." "The people of academic culture, of speculative disengagement and serene intellectual indifference, sided with Erasmus. The moderates throughout Europe, the gentlemen of courts, the semi-skeptical intelligences of the universities, told the golden-mouthed apostle of compromise that he was right.... The heart of Christianity beat with Luther instead."

It is well that the fortunes of the Reformation did not lie with Erasmus. It is a blessed thing that the issues of the American Revolution were not settled by the "Olivebranch Men" who were trying to avoid the "extremism" of the immortal fifty-six who signed the Declaration of Independence.

Joseph Parker said of Charles H. Spurgeon: "The only colors Mr. Spurgeon knew were black and white. In all things he was definite. With Spurgeon you were either up or down, in or out, alive or dead. As for middle zones, graded lines, light compounded with shadow in a graceful exercise of give and take, he only looked upon them as heterodox and as implacable enemies of the Metropolitan Tabernacle." Definitely, Mr. Spurgeon was not a moderatist. In the "downgrade controversy" he was no doubt labeled an extremist by all who traveled the middle of the road. How we need a revival of his "extremism" today!

In these last days when, in advance preparation for Antichrist, all the mountains are being leveled into one plain, middle-of-the-roadism is having a field day. Even the word "square," once synonymous with integrity and honesty, has come to mean an odd number and a freak. Moderatism is the creed of the faceless, the hallmark of the rubber-stamp age. As the world church shapes up toward the day when the harlot rides the beast, all distinctions are disappearing amid religious fogs and doctrinal twilights. It is a great day for Gamaliel and Erasmus and their multiplied progeny who thrive in conditions of low visibility. The man who is really against something and for something, and who dares to be a cipher in a world of zeroes, is in for a rough time. His main opposition, if he is an old-fashioned Christian, will not come from the pagan world without, but from the moderatists within the fold. His worst foes will be those of his own household. God grant him grace in double measure that, having done all, he may stand!

CHAPTER 8

"Must You Live?"

... neither count I my life dear unto myself... (Acts 20:24).

In the days of the early church, Christians had to make a living even as you and I. Some of them carved and gilded images for the pagans. They did not worship these images, of course, nor did they bow in their shrines, but they saw no harm in making and polishing images for sale. Their argument sounds familiar today: "After all, somebody will do it, anyway—and I have to live." Tertullian, one of the giants of that day, answered such an argument with one question: "Must you live?"

Tertullian held that a Christian has only one "must"—he must be faithful to Jesus Christ, come what may, live or die. There were no ifs and reservations and alibis. One did not have to live; he had only to be true to the Master. "We ought to obey God rather than men" (Acts 5:29).

A lot of water has run under the bridge since Tertullian. On Sunday morning multitudes of church members sing:

> Faith of our fathers, holy faith,
> We will be true to thee till death.

Most of them are not true enough to get back to the evening service! Today the issues are about the same as in the early church. If a Christian belonged to a trade guild, he was supposed to go to its orgies. If he did not participate, he might have lost his job. Today we have the boss's Christmas party or some other get-together. Some Christians defend the cocktail by saying, "I must live." Tertullian would ask, "Must you live?" But we are short on Tertullians.

There are clever ways and devious tricks by which modern church members would stay on good terms with both Christ and Belial. In the Roman Empire everybody was expected to put a pinch of incense on the altar and vow allegiance to Caesar. Plenty of Americans would see nothing wrong in that—"You see, I don't really worship Caesar in my heart, but why get into trouble? I don't mind going through the motions to placate the powers that be. Then I will go to church and worship the way I really believe."

The early Christians died rather than offer that incense. They had but one Lord and they loved Him more than life itself. They counted not their lives dear unto themselves. They didn't have to live; they only had to be faithful. Tertullian would have a rough time getting that across to the average American Christian. In this nuclear age, the all-important thing is to stay alive at any cost. Winston Churchill envisioned the day when "safety would be the sturdy child of terror and survival the twin brother of annihilation."

Today we negotiate with Communist gangsters and compromise our national integrity and reverse the American policy of the past—all in an effort to stay alive. Everything is geared to biological survival, as though that were the chief end of life. A small boy was asked, "What do you want to be when you grow up?" He answered, "Alive!"

We did not start out that way. Patrick Henry asked, "Is life so dear, and peace so sweet, as to be purchased at the price of chains and slavery?" He chose liberty or death. Today we must live, liberty or no liberty. The fifty-six signers of the Declaration of Independence risked security for liberty. Today we risk liberty for security and we may end up without either. We are ready to do anything but die. There was a time when some things were more precious than life. Theodore Roosevelt said that among those things which would destroy America was "Safety first instead of duty first."

Tertullian might well ask at a summit conference: "Must you live?" Peace at any price, they say, is better than no peace. Life at any price, they say, is better than not to live. We are obsessed with saving our hides at the cost of our honor, if need be, and we may save neither hides nor honor.

> 'Tis man's perdition to be safe,
> When for the truth he ought to die.

At Munich, Neville Chamberlain learned that "You can't do business with Hitler." The times called for a Churchill. The price for survival is too high to pay. It is better to die for a conviction than to live with a compromise. Self-preservation is a powerful instinct, but it is not the most important thing on earth.

Christians do not have to live; they have only to be faithful to Jesus Christ, not only *until* death but *unto* death if necessary. When a man becomes a Christian, he loses his right to his own life. He is not his own—he is bought with a price. He is the personal property of Jesus Christ, bought and paid for with the blood of Calvary. For him, living and dying are incidental. He is here to glorify Jesus Christ, whether by life or by death. Whether he lives, he lives unto the Lord, or whether he dies, he dies unto the Lord. Whether he lives or dies, he is the Lord's. He counts not his life dear unto himself. To live is Christ and to die is gain. Anything that compromises that all-out devotion is to be refused at any cost. A pinch of incense to Caesar may look innocent enough to others, but to a Christian it is anathema, for he knows but one Lord and he will not, by life or by lip, pay even a gesture of allegiance to another. If a pagan guild would compromise his vows, he would lose his job first. He doesn't have to eat; he has only to be faithful to Jesus Christ.

There are many modern ways of offering incense to Caesar, and polishing idols is a flourishing business in America. The business, social, and entertainment worlds are under the god of this age and they are not friends of grace to help us on to God. To be sure, all of us cannot make a living in businesses operated by Christians. It is not obligatory that the top man in your line be a deacon or that the main office be staffed by Sunday school teachers. We must work in a pagan world and let our light shine in a dark place. But when the setup demands that we carve images or burn incense to Caesar, then we have but one loyalty. If our living, or even our lives, be involved, Tertullian is still up to date: "Must you live?"

There are a thousand angles to this problem. Selling books in a store where filthy literature is part of the stock, waiting on tables in restaurants where liquor is served, playing for dances as a member of the school band—from these to major issues of principle in high position, Tertullian is still up to date. The old argument is still advanced: "After all, I don't run the place. I only work here *and I have to live.*" But Tertullian would ask, "Must you live?"

There are no easy solutions. Sometimes we must cut knots instead of untying them. Radical? Yes, but the early Christians upset the world. Later, when Constantine joined the church and the world, there were no such scruples—and the glory departed.

Of course, there is infinitely more to the Christian life than refusing to gild images or offer incense to Caesar. There must be more than refusing to sell beer or leaving the Sons and Daughters of I Will Arise because they sponsor dances. This is the negative side, but it is there and the New Testament stresses it. We are not only to put on the Lord Jesus; we must make no provision for the flesh. Although the ideal is to be so much in love with Jesus Christ that the world presents no problem, most Christians are not that far along and we need to hear Tertullian thunder his question. The devil has cleverly set up this present age in such a way that what puts butter on our bread too often determines our conduct. We have developed a pleasant, agreeable Christianity, an amiable neutralism that raises no eyebrows at gilding images and offering incense to Caesar. We are like the church at Thyatira where, along with the *agape* of which we hear so much today, there existed a smiling "get-alongism" that allowed Jezebel to set up her altar, bringing the reproof of the Lord.

This world has been moved by "fools for Christ's sake" who count not their lives dear unto themselves. In order to build a popular, prosperous, religious superchurch we have thrown open

the doors to unconverted pagans. In order to create a huge ecclesiastical empire we burn incense to Caesar. But God is taking out
a remnant, marshaling a Master's minority at the end of the age,
love-slaves of Jesus Christ who do not have to live but only to be
faithful. Like Paul, they are not here to survive but to serve: "...
to abide in the flesh is more needful for you" (Philippians 1:24).
All that matters is that Christ be magnified, whether by life or
by death. We are here not for survival or success, but for stew-
ardship, and it is required of stewards only that they be found
faithful.

Such a Christian has nothing, yet he possesses all things.
Satan can give him nothing, for he possesses all things. Satan
can take nothing from him, for he does not have anything. Satan
may kill him, but to die is gain. I have read of a Coast Guard
crew summoned on a stormy night to rescue survivors from a
sinking vessel. One member of the crew was fearful: "Captain,"
he moaned, "we'll never get back." "We don't have to come back,"
was the reply; "we only have to go." That sounds like Tertullian
again. It is true faith which is "not belief in spite of evidence but
life in scorn of consequence."

Paul did not say, "I count not my life dear." Life is dear and
precious in God's sight. Paul said, "I count not my life dear *unto
myself.*" There are two ways of counting not life dear unto oneself.
Every few days we read of a carful of teenagers at the end of a
wild ride, a horribly scrambled mass of flesh and glass and steel.
That is sin's way—the devil's way—of counting not life dear to
oneself. That is "living dangerously"—the wrong way.

There is another way. The body of Jim Elliot in Ecuador was
another mangled sight when the savages were through with him.
But his soul went marching home through gates of splendor. He
counted not his life dear unto himself. That is Christ's way, Paul's
way, the Christian way. That is "living dangerously"—for God.
One need not be a martyr at savage hands to do that. There are
dangers aplenty around us every day, far more subtle and more
devastating to the soul. Amidst them all, we have but one obli-
gation—to magnify Jesus Christ, whether by life or by death, for

whether we live or die, we are the Lord's. We do not have to live; we have only to be faithful.

CHAPTER 9

Foretaste of Glory

And... tasted the good word of God, and the powers of the world to come (Hebrews 6:5).

The Scriptures tell us that the Christian can have a foretaste of glory and a preview of Paradise before he gets there. The present age is a failure. The first Adam started out with all creation at peace, but he fell and creation became a wreck. The reign of tooth and claw began and we are to blame because we listened to Satan. The earth is still beautiful in spots, even in its ruined condition, but it is only a marred and broken image of what it was and what it shall be.

The first Adam failed, but God sent His Son, the second Adam, to be the first of a new race: "As many as received him, to them gave he power to become the sons of God, even to them that believe on his name" (John 1:12). The greatest race question is this: Do I belong only to the race of the first Adam, or am I a member of the new race, the children (as well as the creation) of God, through faith in Jesus Christ?

The Scriptures promise a redeemed earth and a new age when our Lord returns to reign. The whole creation is "on tiptoe," as Dr. J. B. Phillips puts it, earnestly expecting the day when the sons of God come into their own. Dr. A. T. Robertson wrote, "This mystical sympathy of physical nature with the work of grace is beyond the comprehension of most of us. But who can disprove it?" John Keble wrote:

> It was not then a poet's dream,
> An idle vaunt of song,

61

Such as beneath the moon's soft beam
Or vacant fancies throng,
Which bids me see in heaven or earth,
In all fair things around,
Strong yearnings for a blest new birth
With sinless glories crowned.

It is not mere fancy to sense, as some often do, perhaps at sundown or while listening to a birdsong at twilight, or in the holy hush of a starry night, a longing beyond words to express, as though all creation were sighing for a better day.

The Christian has already tasted of the powers of the age to come. He got his first taste when he was born again. The assurance of salvation is, as Fanny Crosby put it, "a foretaste of glory divine." The presence of the Holy Spirit gives us an earnest, a pledge, a first installment of more to follow, here and hereafter. In prayer, in Christian fellowship, in feeding upon the Word, in a score of ways we sample in advance what will be our regular fare through all eternity.

The hill of Zion yields a thousand sacred sweets
Before we reach the heavenly fields or walk the golden streets.

The trees of the age to come extend their branches over the wall on this side and we may enjoy some of their fruits here and now. God has not reserved everything for the next world, like packages not to be opened until after death. "Entered Into Rest" was not meant to be an epitaph.

When I was a boy, booksellers used to offer their customers a prospectus, the covers and sample pages of the complete book. It was calculated to awaken an appetite for the whole volume. The crumbs made you want the cake! God offers us even now a prospectus of that which is to come. All of the pages are not there—our eyesight is weak and our understanding limited—but we can enjoy the prospectus before we get to the heavenly library to read the never-ending book. Only of the age to come can it be said:

Then we shall be where we would be;
Then we shall be what we should be;
Things that are not now nor could be
Soon shall be our own.

Nevertheless, we can have a limited enjoyment of that blessed age and "reign *in life*" *before* we reign with our Lord in eternity. I would not presume to say how much of the age to come we may appropriate in advance. A little tenement child who had never had enough to eat was placed in a hospital. When a nurse brought in a glass of rich milk the famished youngster took a few swallows and then asked, "How deep may I drink?" Alas, we are sippers and nibblers when we should eat and drink of the heavenly fare! We seem to be afraid to take deep draughts of what God has provided in Christ Jesus. Dr. A. J. Gordon asks, "And who can tell what may not happen when a Christian *who has not learned to doubt* comes to God to claim the fulfillment of one of His promises?" I would not dare to say how much a Christian may claim for body, mind, and spirit, even in this age before the new day dawns. I am sure that we can have as much as we need to do what God wants us to do for as long as He wants us to do it. That is far more than most of us have dared to claim! Among the things Paul lists as belonging to the Christian are "things to come." We do not have to die before we can enjoy any of that. There is much fruit available on "the branches over the wall." There are now more pages available in the prospectus. Most of the "thousand sacred sweets" are still untouched. There is more for us here and now than a foretaste of glory. This glorious present provision is bounded only by God's will, our need, and our faith. Within that glorious range there is as much as our faith will take and our vessels will hold.

When our Lord was on earth He demonstrated the powers of the age to come. In His miracles we have glorious flashes of that day when we shall live free from all the limitations of this earth. The Saviour is not walking our roads in a visible body today, but He lives in the hearts of all who trust Him. The Christian lives a supernatural life in this natural world and there are special experiences when he may taste to an unusual degree the powers of the coming age. There may be a touch of the body, an illumination of the mind, a quickening of the spirit in which we are granted a foretaste of glory even above our average daily experience. The Christian is an heir to a better world and he can begin to "cash in" on his inheritance now. Let us not live like paupers when we are children of the King!

This "present enjoyment of the future" means living in Kingdom Come before it arrives. Of course the Kingdom of God is already here as a spiritual reality wherever God reigns in the hearts of men; but it will be a visible Kingdom when our Lord returns. When we taste the powers of that coming age, we anticipate that glorious day. Dr. A. J. Gordon wrote, "The age to come is the resurrection age, the time of the redemption of the body. We know the powers of that age not simply by prediction and promise but by experience. Every miracle is a foretaste thereof, a sign of its universal healing and restitution. The driftwood and floating vegetation which met the eye of Columbus as he was keeping lookout upon his ship assured him of the proximity of the new world which he was seeking. His study of geography had convinced him of the existence of that world. But now he tasted its powers, he saw and handled its actual firstfruits. So it is with us voyagers to the world to come, the millennial age, and the time of the restitution of all things. As those who have known and credited our Lord's miracles while on earth or have experienced the wonders of recovery which He has wrought as He still stretches out His hand to heal, we have tasted the powers of the coming age."

It is for this blessed age that creation longs (Romans 8:19). Johann Goethe wrote, "Often have I had the sensation as if nature in wailing sadness entreated something of me so that not to understand what she longed for cut me to the heart." And not only creation but we ourselves who enjoy these firstfruits of the Spirit long for that day (Romans 8:23). In fact we are often longing when we could be living in the present enjoyment of what is to be our full portion later. Let us not be sighing when we could be singing!

Foretaste of glory! Living in Kingdom Come! It is the glorious privilege of every child of God and there is no telling how many fruits we may feed upon from the branches over Zion's wall before we ever enter the portals. We used to sing, "O land of rest, for thee I sigh," and indeed we do, but there is a preliminary rest available here and now whereby we carry our vacation inside instead of hunting a haven in the mountains or by the shore. It is a preview and prospectus of Paradise in God's gracious provision for us weary travelers in these lowlands—which Matthew Henry rightly called "our passage and not our portion." We are headed for a better country, the land of our heavenly citizenship, and we may sample its delights far in advance. Have you tasted the powers of the age to come?

CHAPTER 10

"... So Send I You"

... as my Father hath sent me, even so send I you (John 20:21).

While preaching in a small midwestern city I stayed in a hotel that displayed in its lobby a poster depicting the local civic attractions. Industry, schools, the library, the business section—all were represented, and along with them one of the churches. I couldn't help thinking that in the days of the early church the Jerusalem Chamber of Commerce never would have included the Christian meeting-place among their boasted features. That hated sect was too big a nuisance and stirred up too much commotion to be listed with pride by the city fathers. Christians kept Jerusalem in turmoil and nobody would have thought of classing them among the civic assets.

Before Pentecost, however, the early disciples showed few signs of turning the world upside down. John tells us that the risen Lord found one band of His followers behind closed doors, "for fear of the Jews..." (John 20:19). Their Master had been slain and they were next in line, so they hid themselves. The church today, for the most part, is behind closed doors for fear—fear of communism, fear of catastrophe, fear of the consequences of being really Christian. We are a timid church in a tortured world. Someone has said, "What bothers me is not the wolfishness of the devil's wolves but the sheepishness of the Lord's sheep." We are not only *behind* closed doors but *before* closed doors the world around: the Iron Curtain, the Bamboo Curtain, all kinds of curtains. It is a day of closed doors.

Yet the risen Lord appeared to His frightened disciples and said, "Peace be unto you..." (John 20:21). He showed them the wounds in His hands and side and they were glad when they saw the Lord. Then He gave them a commission: "... as my Father hath sent me, even so send I you" (John 20:21). He had said earlier, in His high-priestly prayer before the crucifixion, "As thou hast sent me into the world, even so have I also sent them into the world" (John 17:18).

When Jesus came into this world He found it a very unfriendly place. When He was born, King Herod tried to kill Him in the slaughter of the little children. All the days of His earthly ministry His enemies argued with Him, held worried conferences, plotted to destroy Him, and made attempts on His life. He lived through a storm of bitter hostility that reached its climax when the religious leaders seized Him and a howling mob demanded His death. He was beaten and crowned with thorns and died in the horrors of a brutal and bloody crucifixion. Now, risen from the dead, He stands among His fearful followers, shows them His wounds, and sends them out into the same world that treated Him with such vile contempt. And it is into this same world that He sends us who believe in Him, every one of us, today.

The world has not improved in its attitude toward Jesus Christ. True, we have had almost two thousand years of Christianity and the gospel has made its impact, but the world is still under the power of Satan. It hates Jesus Christ and would crucify Him again. The notion has gotten around that humanity is more kindly disposed toward Him today. Much of what we hear at Christmas time about peace and good will would give that impression, but a lot of what gets mixed up with the holly and tinsel and paganism of Christmas is a parody on what the Babe of Bethlehem really came to this world to do. This age will accept an imitation Christianity that makes no demands and does not condemn sin in the light of the cross, but real Christians today are a persecuted minority in a pagan world. There is quite a fad for making Christianity acceptable, but it is a waste of time. The preaching of the cross is to them that perish foolishness, and someone has said that if that be true, then the preachers of the cross must be to the world fools. Our Lord was popular when He first proclaimed the Kingdom, wrought miracles, and fed the multitudes. But when He began to preach that we must eat His flesh and drink His blood to have His life, the crowd dwindled until He said to His disciples, "Will ye also go away?" (John 6:67). It was not far from the multitude who wanted to crown Him King to the mob who wanted to crown Him with thorns. One day they were for His coronation; a little later they demanded His crucifixion. The modern world is not different. Men are ready to crown a King who will feed them with loaves and fishes, but they are not willing to go with a suffering Saviour the way of the cross. They are ready for a political and social revolution, but not for self-denial and discipleship.

The church, unfortunately, has gone along with the world and we have developed a modified, watered-down Christianity that a worldling can accept without being born again or renouncing his idols. Our Lord sent His disciples out as sheep among wolves; now the wolves are being invited into the sheepfold. We have filled our churches with baptized pagans. The church has become worldly and the world churchly. This is exactly what the devil ordered and he has accomplished more by joining churches than by fighting them.

The early church met the pagan world in a head-on collision and came off the winner, turning the Roman Empire upside down. In this present-day twilight era we are largely shadow-boxing, playing church, carrying on a mock warfare, fighting sham battles. We need to face grim reality. The real issue is absolute Light against absolute darkness, Christ or Antichrist. Our Lord is sending us into a world where the devil has heated the furnace seven times hotter because he knows his time is short. Lawlessness abounds and love abates. If you think this age is favorably disposed toward the gospel and that Christ is more acceptable, you do not know your Bible and you do not know your generation. There are more church members than ever, since it adds to community status and looks good in an obituary; let a man really dare to be a New Testament Christian and take Christ seriously, beginning next Monday morning, and he will wake up to the fact that he is a sheep among wolves.

It is an insane world in moral delirium tremens, a decaying carcass awaiting the vultures of judgment. We are not sent into it to reform it, for it is past reformation. We have not been commissioned to be professional do-gooders, spreading cold cream on cancer and dusting off iniquity with a powder puff. We are here to preach sin black, hell hot, judgment certain, eternity long, and salvation free. We Christians have the biggest business on earth and we are totally inadequate, as helpless as those frightened disciples behind closed doors, for fear. Just as our Lord appeared then and made the difference, He can do it now and get us out of hiding—and sometimes we hide in our costly churches—and out into this mad world to shine our light in the darkness where it is needed, instead of outdazzling each other in indoor religious performances.

How does He qualify us for this mission? How did He do it long ago with those bewildered disciples? He began by saying, "Peace be unto you...." No man is ready to go into the world as a witness for Christ unless and until the Lord has spoken peace to the soul. This is a double peace, a peace *with* God (Romans 5:1), and the peace *of* God that passeth understanding (Philippians 4:7). We experience the first when we first trust the Saviour; the second is ours as we trust Him daily and make our requests known with thanksgiving. The first makes us sure of heaven; the second garrisons our hearts and minds against the vexations of earth. "Peace I leave with you, my peace I give unto you: not as the world giveth, give I unto you" (John 14:27)—that is the legacy He left to us, and it is for everyone, anyone, any time, and all the time.

Long ago, in my first country pastorate, I preached once a week in an old schoolhouse to a gathering of farm folk. One cold February night a dear woman who lived seven miles from the meeting place and had started on foot to the service when someone gave her a ride, stood in the testimony meeting and said, "I thank God for a deep, settled peace. The world didn't give it and the world can't take it away." I wonder how many can truthfully say that these days when mental cases overflow our hospitals and psychiatrists are having a field day? We are not ready to be one of the Saviour's Peace Corps in this world if we do not have His peace in our hearts.

Jesus showed to His disciples His wounded hands and side. He cannot send us into the world until we are identified with Him in His crucifixion. Paul said, "I am crucified with Christ..." (Galatians 2:20). Too many, like Peter, confess the Christ but deny the cross (Matthew 16:16-22). Robert Murray McCheyne wrote, "Men return again and again to the few who have mastered the spiritual secret, whose lives have been hid with Christ in God. These are of the old-time religion, hung to the nails of the cross." Baptism symbolizes this identification but, alas, how few ever understand its meaning! Paul bore in his body the dying of the Lord Jesus (2 Corinthians 4:10) and "the marks of the Lord Jesus" (Galatians 6:17). He said, "Let no one trouble me as to my credentials—here they are!" Today we measure God's ministers by diplomas, popularity, abilities, prestige. Our Lord looks for scars, not medals. A week after His appearance to the disciples, our Lord appeared again and Thomas was convinced when he saw the Saviour's wounds. God's witnesses must be men of the cross, bringing the message of the cross and wearing the marks of the cross, looking for that day when we shall know Him by the prints of the nails in His hands.

After the risen Saviour spoke His peace and showed His wounds, we read, "Then were the disciples glad, when they saw the Lord" (John 20:20). We are not ready to carry the Good News of the gospel until first the Lord has made us glad. He left us not only a legacy of peace but also a legacy of joy: "These things have I spoken unto you, that my joy might remain in you, and that your joy might be full" (John 15:11). We are bearers of good tidings of great joy and we have no business going out to tell it if our own hearts do not rejoice. Christ does not appear visibly now as He did to the disciples then, but remember that He said to Thomas one week later: "... because thou hast seen me, thou hast believed: blessed are they that have not seen, and yet have believed" (John 20:29)—and Peter echoes it: "Whom having not seen, ye love; in whom, though now ye see him not, yet believing, ye rejoice with joy unspeakable and full of glory" (1 Peter 1:8).

The gospel is not a funeral or a frolic, but it is a feast and a feast is a joyful occasion. One hardly gets the impression from the average church service that we Christians are unusually happy. We look as worried, bewildered, or disinterested as any other aggregation. Sometimes we try to remedy that by artificial stimulation with a whipped-up joy such as a cheer leader arouses at a ballgame. The disciples were glad when they saw the Lord. Maybe we've been looking at each other, which would hardly set us rejoicing! The early church swept the world with a radiant message of victory that could be sung in prison at midnight. The Wesleyan revival transformed England with the songs of Charles Wesley as well as the preaching of his brother John. Those Methodists had something to sing about and it began with a heartwarming when one man saw the Lord and was glad.

Then our Lord commissioned His disciples, saying, "... as my Father hath sent me, even so send I you." Every Christian is commissioned, for every Christian is a missionary. It has been said that the gospel is not merely something to come to church to hear but something to go from church to tell—and we are all appointed to tell it! It has also been said, "Christianity began as a company of lay witnesses; it has become a professional pulpitism, financed by lay spectators." Nowadays we "hire" a church staff to do "full-time Christian work," and we sit in church on Sunday to watch them do it. Every Christian is meant to be in full-time Christian service. Aren't we all called to live for God every hour of the day, every day of the week, every week of the month, every month of the year? There is indeed a special ministry of pastors, teachers, and evangelists—but for what? "For the perfecting of the saints, for the work of the ministry..." (Ephesians 4:12)—for the perfecting of the laymen for *their* ministry!

As the Father sent the Son into the world, the Son has sent us. This does not mean we are sent on a special mission occasionally to do church visitation or help raise the budget. He sends us, once for all, to *live* the en-Christed life in the office or shop or wherever we work for a living, in our social and business life as well as our church life. This is not a part-time job, limited perhaps to being a church deacon or an usher on Sundays. This is our *vocation* and we carry it on while we work at our job or business or profession. We have been called out of this world to go right back into it to win souls out of it—and that is the only business we have in it!

Believe it or not, one thing yet remained before those disciples were ready to go out into the world as witnesses. One may have peace with God and the peace of God; he may be crucified with Christ; he may have his heart filled with joy; he may have a divine commission—and yet not be ready to enter upon his mission. The disciples had walked with Jesus for three years; they had sat at the feet of the greatest of teachers; they were witnesses of His resurrection; yet they were behind closed doors for fear. Something was lacking "... he breathed on them, and saith unto them, Receive ye the Holy Ghost" (John 20:22). This was prophetic, of course, for He had told them to wait until they were endued with power from on high, and that did not happen until Pentecost.

We hear about everything else nowadays in the preparation of Christ's witnesses: training, education, personality, ability, appearance, enthusiasm—everything is emphasized except being filled with the Spirit. We shy away from that as though it were something wild and weird. There has been extremism indeed on this subject, and so has there been on every other doctrine of our faith. We are more inclined to argue about it than to experience it. Whatever it is, most of us do not have it. Yet it is not only the privilege but also the duty of every Christian.

We are filled with the Spirit when we realize our need of it; when we give up everything that stands in the way of it; when we come to Christ in full committal; when we receive and believe we have received. It is a matter of thirsting, coming, drinking, believing, overflowing (John 7:37-39). We Christians are not making much impact today because we are going out into the world in our own strength. It was the Holy Spirit that made the difference between fearful weaklings behind closed doors and fearless witnesses before all Jerusalem. Our Lord made the difference then; He makes the difference still.

Observe, finally, that He sends us into this world with authority: "Whose soever sins ye remit, they are remitted unto them; and whose soever sins ye retain, they are retained" (John 20:23). This is not our authority, but His. We cannot forgive sin. But when we proclaim the gospel and men receive it, we have a right to say to anyone who repents of his sins and trusts the Saviour, "Your sins are forgiven." The authority of the saints rests upon the authority of the Scriptures, the Saviour, and the Spirit.

You will notice that Christ does not say, "... as my Father hath sent me, even so send I you" into the world to entertain it, to philosophize, to teach a better system of ethics. He does not send us out to play around on the circumference, to deal with incidentals. The trouble with this world is sin, and we are sent into it to deal with its trouble. Why did the Father send the Son into the world? To live the ideal life, to teach a higher moral code, to inspire us with a lofty example? No, He was called "Jesus" because He came to save us from *sin,* to give His life a ransom for many, to seek and to save the lost, to die for the sins of the world. He came to deal with the main trouble and He sends us to declare that, once and for all, that trouble has been taken care of on Calvary.

Here then is the need of the church today which hides behind closed doors and stands powerless before closed doors: to have a fresh experience of the risen Lord; to hear His voice speaking peace to our hearts; to see with new understanding His wounded hands and side; to know the gladness that vision brings; to be filled with the Holy Spirit; to hear Him say, "... as my Father hath sent me, so send I you"; to bring to a sin-sick world the only answer to its guilt and shame—the Saviour's Word to all who trust Him: "Thy sins be forgiven thee."

> So send I you to hearts made hard by hatred,
> To eyes made blind because they will not see,
> To spend, tho' it be blood, to spend and spare not....
> So send I you to taste of Calvary.

CHAPTER 11

Growing Goliaths and Developing Davids

Not by might, nor by power, but by my spirit, saith the Lord of Hosts (Zechariah 4:6).

Dr. J. B. Gambrell relates a most interesting incident from General Stonewall Jackson's famous valley campaign. It was necessary for the general to get his army across a river one night, so he gave orders to the engineers to make a way for the artillery and wagons to go over. He also called his wagon-master, who was a blacksmith, to headquarters and gave him instructions to get the wagon train across the river as fast as possible.

The engineers went to work in their usual expert manner to devise a bridge. The blacksmith, knowing only that something was to be done in the most practical way, gathered a force and with logs and rocks and fence rails improvised a bridge. Between midnight and day he awakened General Jackson and said, "General, we have got all the wagons and artillery across." The astonished general asked, "Where are the engineers!" The blacksmith replied, "They're over there in a tent still drawing pictures and planning a bridge."

Never have we had so many experts sitting around drawing pictures and making plans as today. We need a few blacksmiths to get us over the river.

The present-day situation, both in the world of nations and in religion, is very much like that of the Israelites facing the Philistines with their Goliath strutting back and forth. I am sure that the top-brass Israelites spent every day discussing ways and means to deal with the giant and defeat the Philistines. Then, one day, little David came along and it was all over.

Today the free world is lined up against the hordes of communism and Goliath is on parade. The nations of the West are huddled in fear, confusion, and uncertainty. We have been maneuvered into an inferiority complex. Our foreign policy is based on fear. Experts spend their time in Washington, Geneva, and elsewhere wrangling over what to do. Engineers are drawing the prettiest pictures of bridges ever produced. What we need is a blacksmith to get us over the river.

We spend our time imitating the Russians, which puts us in second place and is very embarrassing. A prilgrimage to Russia has become a "must" on the program of politicians and other professions. We are considered backnumbers, unqualified even to mention the subject if we haven't had three days in Moscow. Vice Admiral Hyman Rickover said, "If the Russians announced that they were going to send a man to hell, there would be at least two government agencies before the Appropriations Commission of Congress tomorrow with their public-relations men asking for money on the grounds, 'We've got to get there first.'"

The effect on us and our allies is devastating. We make ourselves ridiculous by playing up to Moscow. We have conferred on communism a dignity (which it does not have) and have made it respectable (which it is not) by sitting at tables with gangsters as though they were gentlemen, forgetting that there is no honor among thieves. We might as well confer with the underworld on law and order as to talk peace on earth with the Communists.

If the Israelites had waited until they could grow a giant as big as Goliath, they would still be pitched by the Valley of Elah. Deliverance did not lie in that direction. The answer was not in growing a Goliath but in developing a David, and that was exactly what God was doing in the solitudes around Bethlehem.

The religious world, like the world of nations, is in a dilemma like that of the Israelites of old. We are up against not only communism, but materialism, unbelief, godlessness, and anarchy drawn up in battle array. Not one but a dozen Goliaths swagger back and forth saying of us, as Joel puts it, "Where is their God?" (2:17). Some are calling this "the post-Christian era."

Mohammedanism and Hinduism are having revivals; in fact, almost everything is having a revival except Christianity. It is a desperate hour. To use Dr. Gambrell's illustration again, Christian experts aplenty are studying maps and planning bridges. We need a blacksmith to get us over the river.

Going back to the Israelites and Philistines, we are more interested in growing Goliaths than in developing Davids. We are occupied more with the strategy of the Philistines than with the Spirit of God. We are more excited over how the business world does it, how the social world does it, how the entertainment world does it, than with how God does it. We have become copy-cats, which gives us an inferiority complex and defeats us from the start. We are spending our time studying Goliath's armor and how to duplicate it instead of studying the secret of David's sling and stone. The victory is won "Not by might, nor by power, but by my spirit, saith the Lord of Hosts" (Zechariah 4:6)—not by the mighty, but by the Almighty.

This age makes much of scholarship, specialization, and showmanship. These are the weapons of the modern Philistines and we are trying to defeat them with their own equipment. Scholarship is not enough. We need sanctified scholarship and can use all the brains we can accumulate. I have heard of a brother who said in his prayer, "Lord, I thank Thee that I am ignorant." Someone remarked, "Evidently he has a lot to be thankful for!" God puts no premium on ignorance. However, we have never had more education and less sense than today.

Evangelical Christianity is blowing a fuse trying to sound intellectual. We have developed an apologetic attitude in the presence of liberalism. We seem to be saying, "Pardon us, we don't know much, but give us time and we will try to catch up with our homework and develop some scholars who can match wits with the best of them." The new theology is a pitiful example of nervous orthodoxy. Conservatives spend much of their time merely trying to explain that they are not fundamentalists! We shall have to produce something besides more Ph.D.'s to solve our problem. We are not going to think ourselves out of this dilemma, for the way out is not head-first!

Specialization is not enough. The history of Christianity proves that while engineers and experts were drawing pictures and planning bridges, God has raised up blacksmiths from time to time to get us over the river.

Years ago a convention met in Indianapolis to discuss "How to Reach the Masses." One day during that convention a young man stood on a box on a street corner and began to preach. He gathered a crowd which he led down to the Academy of Music where he preached to them again. But he had to cut short that service, for the convention on "How to Reach the Masses" was soon to gather in the same auditorium. While the convention was discussing how to reach the masses, the young man, who was Dwight L. Moody, was doing it! It was a case of the engineers and the blacksmith all over again. I am sure that there were experts and strategists in the Israelite army, but it remained for a shepherd boy with substandard equipment to slay Goliath. This does not mean that it is not important to draw blueprints of bridges; it does mean that God's blacksmiths usually get the job done while experts discuss how to do it.

Showmanship is not enough. Glamour boys with a dash of Hollywood, plenty of public relations, and a superabundance of doubletalk are no match for Goliath. We have had a wave of all that and it has not slain many giants. We have had "an epidemic of amateurism." We have seen youthful satellites go up like rockets and come down like rocks. Some of them have cracked up and dropped out of the race while the tortoise has outrun the hare. Our hearts go out to them; they meant well, but you cannot meet Goliath with gimmicks and glamour.

When some of these scholars, specialists, and showmen get together, they often make ordinary men feel inferior and self-conscious. Dr. Gambrell said, "We are almost dazed with the magnificence of some of their conceptions, and their methods are so fine that the common man feels he does not know where to begin." More than one grass-roots preacher has gone home discouraged and bewildered after the glittering performance of some of these stars. They have said, "I never could be that scholarly. I am not a specialist. I cannot put on a show." Instead of being inspired, they feel like country boys come to town, embarrassed and out of place.

Well, David was a country boy when he arrived at the camp of Israel. When he had his first look at Goliath, he did not lament that Israel had no such giants. He said, "I can handle him. I've had a little practice on a lion and a bear, and this Philistine looks like the next item on my program." David's brothers made fun of him. When God raises up a man, his own brothers and sometimes his fellow preachers may belittle him. Even the brothers of our Lord did not believe in Him.

When the spies returned from exploring Canaan, the majority reported, in effect: "The land is according to plans and specifications, but there are giants over there and we were as grasshoppers in their sight." That is one way of looking at it. When Dwight Moody returned from his preaching mission to the British Isles and was asked how he felt in the presence of those learned divines who attended his meetings, he replied, "They looked like grasshoppers." That is another way of looking at it. Moody was not a scholar, a specialist, or a showman, but he was a blacksmith who built a bridge across the river.

The disciples did not sit around after Pentecost saying, "We are fishermen and unknown men. We don't have a chance. We are no match for scribes and Pharisees." There was not a scholar, a specialist, or a showman in the outfit that turned the world upside down!

When our Lord fed the multitude, there was first a problem of bread: "Whence shall we buy bread, that these may eat?" (John 6:5). Then there was a proposed budget; Philip suggested that two hundred pennyworth of bread would not be enough. Finally there was the provision of a boy: "There is a lad here..." (v. 9). Our Lord did not need a budget; He needed a boy. I will venture that the Israelites facing the Philistines wore out a lot of pencils figuring a budget. But God did not put Goliath out of business with a budget; He used a boy.

What did David do when he walked into that situation? For one thing, he did not clutter himself up with a lot of unnecessary paraphernalia. He did try on Saul's armor, but he put it off and decided to be natural. Ready-made clothes are popular with people of average size; when God raises up a David He does not fit him out in Saul's arsenal. We are so overstocked with our own equipment that the traveler is lost in the baggage. Sometime ago I saw a bird-watcher lugging three cameras, two pairs of binoculars, and several books. He couldn't watch the birds for keeping up with his bird-watching equipment. I will not elaborate on the application. Dr. Gambrell said, "I am dead sure that very much of the religious paraphernalia today cumbers the work it is intended to help." Saul's armory works overtime fitting preachers with ready-made outfits. Once in a while God raises up a David who does better in his own garb and lets Goliath furnish the sword for his own execution. Of course God has used men in armor, too. God did not use David merely because he refused Saul's panoply.

In the second place, David did not propose a summit conference with the Philistines, nor did he offer to "talk it over" with Goliath. We are trying to live these days in an impossible state known as "peaceful coexistence" with the Communists and, in the religious world, at a compromise with the world, the flesh, and the devil. We have developed a generation of diplomats, instead of soldiers, specializing on how to live at a truce with our adversaries. David knew no substitute for victory over Goliath. It was "get or be got." The Bible says, "Resist the devil..." (James 4:7), not "Talk it over with him."

Not long before World War II, Prime Minister Chamberlain met Hitler at Munich. Mr. Chamberlain was a fine, sincere man who wanted peace—and who doesn't?—but he learned that he couldn't do business with Hitler. What was needed then was not a Chamberlain but a Churchill. The armies of the Lord today are trying to patch things up with the Philistines. But you can't talk it over with Goliath. You cannot do business with the devil.

Finally, David understood the nature of the conflict and acted accordingly. He declared that Goliath had defied the armies of the living God, not only the armies of Israel. We must understand the status of our enemy today: he is not only our enemy but the enemy of our God. David faced the mighty in the name of the Almighty: "I come to thee in the name of the Lord of hosts, the God of the armies of Israel, whom Thou hast defied" (1 Samuel 17:45). This stripling was so sure of his God that he said, "This day will the Lord deliver thee into mine hand; and I will smite thee, and take thine head from thee; and I will give the carcases of the host of the Philistines this day unto the fowls of the air, and to the wild beasts of the earth; that all the earth may know that there is a God in Israel" (v. 46). Mind you, not that all the earth might know that there was a *David* in the camp, but that there was a *God* in Israel! David was not out to show himself strong in God's behalf; God was out to show Himself strong in David's behalf.

The crowning statement comes last: "The battle is the Lord's..." (v. 47). We have thought that it is fundamentalism's battle today, orthodoxy's battle, or Christianity's battle; it is the Lord's battle and "they that be with us are more than they be with them" (2 Kings 6:16). We are prone to overestimate our adversary and underestimate our ally. God and David had come to an understanding on the hills of Bethlehem. When a man makes alliance with the Almighty, giants look like grasshoppers.

My brethren, be not fearful of Goliaths who strut around in the camp of the Philistines, mocking the people of God. Be not embarrassed by those of our own number who try to match Goliath's armor or grow giants the size of the adversary. Throw away your inferiority complex in the presence of scholars, specialists, and showmen. (They do some good, for even Saul slew his thousands.) Get alone with God on some Bethlehem hill and come to an agreement. Then go forth with sling and stone, and let Saul keep his armor. Remember that "the battle is the Lord's" and that you are out to demonstrate not David but "that all the earth may know that there is a God in Israel." And I would say to you, as Saul to David, "Go, and the Lord be with thee" (1 Samuel 17:37).

CHAPTER 12

The Four-Hundred-and-First Prophet

Is there not here a prophet of the Lord besides, that we might enquire of him? (1 Kings 22:7).

There is no period of Bible history more dramatic than the life and times of Ahab. Some of the worst and some of the best Old Testament characters were his contemporaries. There was Jezebel, one of the wickedest women who ever lived, and there was Elijah, who lived in a tempest and went to heaven in a whirlwind. The times were evil but they were not dull. Something was happening every minute.

On one occasion, Ahab planned a campaign against Ramoth-gilead. It was a case of a bad man doing a good thing in the wrong way. He had Scripture for the undertaking (Deuteronomy 4:43), but it takes more than a verse to justify such a venture. Ahab inveigled King Jehoshaphat of Judah into joining him in the enterprise. Jehoshaphat was a good man but easily influenced. Ahab put on a banquet—a kick-off supper is usually all it takes to line up a Jehoshaphat. The King of Judah had no business in such a project, and the prophet Jehu asked him, "Shouldest thou help the ungodly, and love them that hate the Lord?" (2 Chronicles 19:2). That text ought to be brought out of the moth balls and put into circulation!

Jehoshaphat asked that the Israelites enquire of the Lord. It was a little late, since they had already made up their minds, but four hundred false prophets were called in and they were unanimous in their opinion. When four hundred preachers agree, there may be grounds for suspicion. Jehoshaphat asked, "Is there not here a prophet of the Lord *besides,* that we may enquire of him?" Give him credit at least for raising the issue: "Isn't there somebody around who speaks for God?" Ahab replied, "There is yet one man..." (1 Kings 19:8). Thank God, there usually is! Ahab added, "... but I hate him"—which is to the eternal credit of that one man—"because he doth not prophesy good concerning me, but evil" (v. 8). Does that not remind us of the Greatest Prophet of all, who said, "... me it [the world] hateth, because I testify of it, that the works thereof are evil" (John 7:7).

While a messenger went to bring Micaiah, one of the false prophets put a theatrical touch on his prophecy and added a dash of Hollywood. Zedekiah waved horns and dramatized the success of the forthcoming venture. It is bad enough to be a false prophet, but to be a ham actor besides is too much.

It was a day of unification, with Ahab and Jehoshaphat uniting; it was a day of *unanimity,* with four hundred prophets in unison; it was a day of *uniformity.* The messenger advised Micaiah that the clergy had agreed and that he should go along with them. But Micaiah had not been regimented, standardized, collectivized, or brainwashed. He had no axe to grind. He was not riding the bandwagon. He was not on his way up. The grass did not look greener in the next pasture and he craved no man's bishopric. He was not a link in anybody's chain.

Joseph Parker said, "The world hates the four-hundred-and-first prophet." Micaiah was Number 401. He broke the monotony when he said, "As the Lord liveth, what the Lord saith unto me, that will I speak" (1 Kings 22:14). He was put on a diet of bread and water, but better a prophet on bread and water than a politician at the feasts of Ahab. With his immortal words Micaiah answered the question of Jehoshaphat: he was the prophet of the Lord *besides.*

We live in days not unlike the times of Micaiah. It is a time of *unification.* Ahab and Jehoshaphat are still going up against Ramoth-gilead. The world is being unified into the world state, the churches into the world church. It is a time of *unanimity,* of yes-men and rubber stamps. Adlai Stevenson is reported to have said that he had devised a new word, "yo," which can mean either "yes" or "no"! It is a time of *uniformity.* We are like eggs in a crate. We talk about being "different" but never have we been more alike. Teenagers boast of being different but they dress alike, talk alike, look alike. The human race is gradually being homogenized into one faceless, monolithic mass. It is the day of the lowest common denominator, the happy medium, the middle of the road. A pleasant "get-alongism," a "togetherness," has so paralyzed us into moral inertia that it is almost impossible to arouse us from our amiable stupor. The steamroller is flattening all the mountains into one level plain. Such a time does not breed prophets.

Men who speak for God never merge into the fog around them. Noah stood alone in a civilization of culture and progress. His contemporaries must have laughed at him as an eccentric who was building an oversized houseboat and looking for the world to end. Elijah stood alone among the priests of Baal and the stooges who ate at Jezebel's table. When he challenged the multitude, that fifth-amendment crowd "answered not a word." Amos stood alone in the religio-political system of his day. Dr. Kyle Yates wrote, "His time had not been spent in a divinity school. He was unwilling to be classed as a member of the guilds who made their living by bowing to the wishes of the people and preaching a pleasing message that would guarantee a return engagement." Jeremiah stood alone among the tranquilizers of his day who were preaching peace when there was no peace; but we are still reading Jeremiah while the happiness boys of his day have been forgotten. Daniel spoke for God in the midst of a pagan empire and it was worth a night in a lion's den to be able to read God's handwriting on the wall. Paul conferred not with flesh and blood but got his orders direct from Headquarters. He was not the product of any assembly line. Dr. Mordecai Ham said, "Paul was a strategist who thought out his strategy on the field of war, not in some Jerusalem war office where parchment and sealing wax were more plentiful than experience and foresight."

True prophets are solitary people; eagles do not fly in flocks. It is not easy to be a Lone Dissenter. When the messenger was sent for Micaiah he must have said, in effect, "The clergy have agreed, and you had better make it unanimous. It is quite an honor to speak before two kings and four hundred prophets. What is it getting you to be an odd number? This is a good gravy train and you had better ride it. This is the mood of the hour and you had better get with it." The same subtle pressure today would persuade preachers to get in step with the times and ride the wave of the future. What we need are more preachers out of step with the times, more odd prophets like Micaiah. We are told that we must adjust. Adjust to what? What is there in this world set-up to adjust to? God's man needs to adjust only to God's Word and God's will. It is not the business of the prophet to harmonize with the times. "What concord hath Christ with Belial?" (2 Corinthians 6:15). The preacher is a soloist; he was never meant to play the accompaniment to anything. The pulpit is not a platform from which to boost the projects of men to bring in a false millennium, the Kingdom without the King. No matter how much Scripture may be quoted or how many false prophets bid Ahab go up against Ramoth-gilead, Micaiah will stand his ground and refuse to be swept off his feet by popular movements. The greatest need of the hour is a four-hundred-and-first prophet of the Lord *besides,* that we may enquire of him.

There are several ways of silencing a prophet. *Persecution* will do it. John the Baptist's head is not always brought in on a charger; there are newer ways of decapitating the prophet with more finesse. *Promotion* sometimes does it. The prophet is given a high seat in the synagogue and is never heard from again. The pressure of the times and discouragement can do it. Jeremiah wanted to quit preaching, get out in the wilderness, and run a motel. *Another prophet* can sometimes do it, as when the prophet at Bethel backslid in his own revival, and he who could turn down a king was deceived by another prophet.

Prophets are not popular at home; they are without honor in their own countries. They are not popular with politicians. Ahab hated Micaiah—but he feared him enough to disguise himself when he went to battle, lest Micaiah's predictions came true.

There was another prophet by the name of Obadiah who was out with Ahab looking for grass when he should have been with Elijah praying for rain. The true prophet does not know how to work both sides of the street. He refuses to dine with Jeroboam and does not let his hair down with the priests of Bethel.

Prophets are not popular with Pharisees. Our Lord asked, "Which of the prophets have not your fathers persecuted?" (Acts 7:52), and He said, "... ye are the children of them that killed the prophets" (Matthew 23:31). One generation stones prophets and the next builds sepulchers in their honor.

> Seven wealthy towns contend for Homer dead,
> Through which the living Homer begged his bread.

Joseph Parker said, "There are those today who would clap their hands at the name of Bunyan who would not admit a living Bunyan to fellowship." Organized religion hates the preacher whose headquarters is heaven, whose Superintendent is God. They are enraged when they cannot control him. The times are never propitious for the Lone Dissenter.

Naturally, one can hardly expect a sermon on Micaiah to be any more popular than its subject. But it is worth preaching if in the congregation one man will hear and heed the call to be a New Testament prophet. If such a prospect is reading this, God bless you. The odds will be four hundred to one, the diet may be bread and water, and the orders are: "What the Lord saith unto me, that will I speak." If you are interested in the prophetic ministry, get ready for trouble! You will be despised by Amaziah and all who want to preserve the status quo at Bethel. You will be hated by Jezebel and all who would set up the worship of Baal alongside the altar of Jehovah. You will be too angular to fit the Procrustean beds of the religious world. You will not be able to feather your nest in this world; scant provision is made for prophets down here. You will report to Heavenly Headquarters and get your orders from the Main Office. If you are a prospect, think it over. You had better mean business, else your ministry will be pathetic instead of prophetic. And remember that prophets are needed but not wanted.

It is time for another four-hundred-and-first prophet of the Lord *besides*, that we might enquire of him.

CHAPTER 13

Have You Lost the Wonder?

And said, Verily I say unto you, Except ye be converted; and become as little children, ye shall not enter into the kingdom of heaven (Matthew 18:3).

Gypsy Smith, the great evangelist, died on a journey in true Gypsy tradition in his eighty-seventh year. Called to preach at seventeen, he was simple and original and colorful. He said, "I was born in a field; don't put me in a flowerpot." He was not a theologian; he would have agreed with Sam Jones, who said he liked flowers but not botany, religion but not theology. He was in a class with Billy Sunday, who used to say that he didn't know any more about theology than did a jack rabbit about ping-pong. When he was advised to learn how to sing from his diaphragm, Gypsy replied that he didn't want to sing from his diaphragm but from his heart.

When asked about the secret of his freshness and vigor, even into old age, he said, *"I have never lost the wonder."* A preacher should have the mind of a scholar, the heart of a child, and the hide of a rhinoceros. His biggest problem is how to toughen his hide without hardening his heart. Gypsy Smith had the heart of a child. He never lost the wonder.

Is not this one thing our Lord meant when He said, "Except ye be converted, and become as little children, ye shall not enter into the kingdom of heaven" (Matthew 18:3)? Children have not lost the wonder. They have not been here long enough to get used to it. They still have a sense of surprise—anything may happen, everything is new. At five they have all the questions, and at eighteen they know all the answers. With a child, every turn of the road may hold a glad discovery. The commonest, most humdrum day is glorified by the glamour of imagination, for life is one-fourth fact and three-fourths fancy.

All too soon, and sooner now than ever, children lose the wonder. A popular magazine inquired recently, "What happened to the Magic of Childhood?" Youngsters become cynical, fed up, sophisticated before they reach their teens. In a television age they have already seen everything. What could possibly surprise them? Recently, in a Mennonite settlement, I read this motto: "We are too soon oldt and too late schmart." "Too smart too soon" would describe the plight of modern youth.

Youth is not entirely to blame. Oldsters have no time to wonder, to reflect, to meditate about anything. We must always be "doing something." There is no time to walk in the woods, to sit before an open fire, "just thinking." Everything is organized, supervised, planned, programmed, and correlated. We don't walk—we take organized hikes. We don't wander along, watching birds—we join a club and keep records. We lose the wonder of it in the work of it.

This gets into Christian experience. What should be a life of faith working by love becomes high-pressure "religious activity." What should be a Thessalonian work of faith and a labor of love and a patience of hope becomes just Ephesian work and labor and patience.

We lose the wonder because too many Christians become childish instead of childlike. They are spiritual babies who won't grow up; milk-feeders who should be on meat; carnal believers, not newborn babes desiring the sincere milk of the Word; overgrown babies who keep pastors busy with a milk bottle. We are not to be "children, tossed to and fro, and carried about with every wind of doctrine, by the sleight of men, and cunning craftiness, whereby they lie in wait to deceive; But speaking the truth in love, [we] may grow up into him in all things, which is the head, even Christ" (Ephesians 4:14-15). We ought to grow up and out of childishness into childlikeness. This secret is kept from the wise and prudent and revealed unto babes. There is not so much to learn as to unlearn. A revival comes when childish church members become childlike in simple faith and obedience.

A childlike Christian does not lose the wonder. There ought to be in every child of God a sense of surprise, a glad expectancy. This is his Father's world and anything can happen. We live on a miracle level and faith is not believing that God *can,* but that He *will* do wonderful things. But we do not look for miracles, and we do not see many. We pray for rain, and do not carry our umbrellas. We ought never to start for a meeting without saying, "This may be the great night!" We get used to being Christians; we take it for granted and we lose the wonder. We work at it harder than ever, but we are shorn Samsons in treadmills. "Christian activity" becomes a battle of wits and a bustle of works. Nothing else under the sun can be as dry, flat, tedious, and exhausting as religious work without the wonder. We dread going to church. We are bored by the sermon. The Sunday school lesson puts us to sleep. Church visiting is drudgery and singing in choir a chore. We are weary in well-doing. Once we stood amazed in the presence of Jesus the Nazarene; now we want to sit amused. Once we were edified; now we must be entertained. It is all work and no wonder.

A passenger on a long train trip was so enthralled by the journey that every few moments he was heard to say, "Wonderful!" The passing scenery, the faces of the fellow passengers, even the smallest details elicited from him glad expressions of keen enjoyment. Finally one traveler, overcome by curiosity, asked him, "How is it that while the rest of us are worn out with this monotonous trip, you are having the time of your life and you keep saying, 'Wonderful!'" He answered, "Until a few days ago, I was a blind man. A great doctor has just given me my sight and what is ordinary to the rest of you is 'out of this world' to me."

If the Great Physician has opened our eyes; if we have been to Siloam's Pool and have come back seeing, if we have had the touch by which we no longer see men as trees walking—if all that has happened to us, why shouldn't we make our way through this poor world singing?

Wonderful, wonderful, Jesus is to me,
Prince of Peace, Counsellor, Mighty God is He;
Saving me and keeping me from all sin and shame,
He is my Redeemer, praise His Name!

CHAPTER 14

Resigned or Re-signed?

Then I said, I will not make mention of him, nor speak any more in his name. But his word was in mine heart as a burning fire shut up in my bones, and I was weary with forbearing, and I could not stay (Jeremiah 20:9).

In this remarkable verse the prophet Jeremiah announces the impossible: he resigns and then declares immediately that he cannot resign; he quits but he cannot quit. Any true preacher can understand Jeremiah's crisis. Almost every man of God has had a spell when he was ready to resign, and knew all the time that he couldn't. A man cannot really preach until preach he must. If he can do something else, he probably should! Paul said, "... woe is unto me, if I preach not the gospel!" (1 Corinthians 9:16). Necessity was laid upon him; he had to do it.

Becoming a minister is not a matter of looking over an assortment of professions—law, medicine, physics, music—and then saying, "I think I'll be a preacher." God is not running a cafeteria where you choose your favorite piece of pie. Jeremiah had a holy bone-fire. He did not merely have to say something—he had something to say. There is a lot of difference between pouring out one's heart and getting something off one's chest. Many a preacher has spent an hour in the pulpit airing his pet grievances under the impression that he was speaking for God. Such men are ready to resign when things don't go their way. A preacher who runs a heavenly fever like Jeremiah's cannot resign, even though nothing goes his way.

We are hearing a lot about how hard it is to be a Christian in these perilous times. We sigh for "the good old days" and paint around them a brighter halo than they deserve. "Say not thou,

93

What is the cause that the former days were better than these? for thou dost not enquire wisely concerning this" (Ecclesiastes 7:10). A subscriber complained to a magazine editor, "Your magazine is not as good as it used to be." The editor replied, "It never has been." When we look at former times, "distance lends enchantment to the view." When was it ever easy to be a Christian? The times have never been propitious. Dr. Phillips says, "Many Christians talk about the difficulties of the times as though we should have to wait for better ones before the Christian religion can take root. It is heartening to remember that this faith took root and flourished amazingly in conditions that would have killed anything less vital in a matter of weeks."

And yet it is true that, as the age draws near to its close, evil is intensified. The devil has pulled out all the stops and stepped up the pressure. But this world is not our rest; it is a training ground for Christian character. You cannot sharpen an axe on a pound of butter.

What is the best way to face this insane age and make our way through this madhouse without going crazy in it? What is a preacher to do when he faces exhaustion in this rat-race? What is he to do when, as Woodrow Wilson once put it, he has worn out his constitution and is living on his by-laws? How is he to carry on in a day when he is a back number if he does not have to his credit (or discredit) one ulcer, one heart attack, or one nervous breakdown?

He can resign. Jeremiah must have had some such inclination when he wrote, "Oh that I had in the wilderness a lodging place of wayfaring men; that I might leave my people, and go from them!" (9:2). He is not the only preacher who has felt like leaving his pulpit to go into the motel business! After all, couldn't he serve the Lord there, testifying to the tourists and giving his money to good causes? At any rate, some have tried such moves and always to their sorrow. Some do their own resigning; others are spared the trouble! Some spend five years resigning while others leave overnight, as though jet-propelled.

There is not much information available on why some preachers quit. One could stock a library with reports of miracles that happened "since I came." They sound like Jonah reporting his campaign in Nineveh. But I have never read much on "why I left." Some leave because they are "Cape Kennedy pastors," using their present pulpits as platforms from which to blast satellites into bigger orbits. Others are simply discouraged, like Matthew Henry who thought his ministry was a failure—and yet he lives on in book shelves and in our hearts today. Some sink into self-pity and lament that they are not appreciated. Blessed is the man who learns quite early that the ministry is the poorest business in the world if one is looking merely for appreciation! After all, a preacher is not to be measured by how many bouquets have been given to him. His ministry may be gauged better by how many brickbats have been pitched at him. Prophets of God have usually been on the receiving end of more mud than medals.

The most miserable men I have known are ministers who have turned in their commissions. Anybody can quit. The church is plagued with quitters, who say, "I go, sir," and go not; who received the Word with joy but have no root and are soon offended. Many sing in the choir for a few weeks and then their feelings are hurt and the nightingale becomes a raven croaking, "Nevermore!" Others come to church for months, and then golf becomes more important than God. Others are church officers until they find out that they cannot run the place, and then they resign because they would rather be Diotrephes loving the preeminence than Demetrius loving the truth. But saddest of all is the preacher who quits preaching. No reward on earth can compensate for that. To be a faithful preacher is no bed of roses, but for a God-called man to become anything else is to try to rest his soul on a bed of thorns. No, the way out is not by resigning.

There is a second possibility for the discouraged minister: *he can become resigned.* He can accept the status quo and go along with it, taking the line of least resistance. Some things are *inevitable,* and a man must face them, even then not with mere resignation because he cannot help himself or with mere submission, but with acceptance, saying with bowed head, "Thy will be done." But there are two ways of saying, "Thy will be done." Some things are not God's will. They are not to be accepted with bowed head in meek resignation. They are wrong and should be changed, and we should face them with heads erect, saying, "Thy will be done—and I'll do my part to see that it is done."

Should we resign ourselves to things as they are and bring our preaching down to suit a generation that cannot endure sound doctrine—all because we have grown weary of holding up a standard to which they do not intend to conform? The worst thing a preacher can do is retreat to his outfit because it refuses to catch up with the standard. Of course it is lonely business out in front. Such a man becomes a target and may be shot at by either the enemy in front or his own regiment behind him.

Life has its inevitables and they are to be met with calm acceptance. It has its impossibles and they are to be faced with common sense. But it also has its inexcusables and they are not to be tolerated with resignation. The early Christians did not adjust to the situation; they adjusted the situation! Martin Luther did not say, "I don't like the way things are going, but I'm not sticking my neck out." John Wesley did not say, "I deplore the deadness of the church, but what can I do about it? I'm not risking my bread and butter on nonconformity." Our forefathers did not resign and quit; neither did they become resigned to the status quo of their day. One thing is certain: they did not trot out that alibi so popular now, "Oh, well, we might as well accept it—these things are here to stay." Of course some conditions are here to stay to the end of the age. So is the devil, so is sin. Liquor is probably here to stay; people are going to drink it and make it and sell it, but that does not excuse legalizing it. Immorality is here to stay, but that is no alibi for making it respectable. "Evil men... shall wax worse and worse..." (2 Timothy 3:13), but that is no justification for coddling criminals and growing sentimental about delinquency. Dancing is here to stay, but that does not mean we must bring it into the church. Television is here to stay, but we need not let it flood our homes with filth because we are too lazy to supervise what we see or let others see.

We live in a day of resignation, not to the inevitable, but to the inexcusable and unjustifiable. In the international realm we are resigned to communism with our policy of appeasement, compromise, and peaceful coexistence in hopeless toleration of what should have been isolated and quarantined like smallpox. "Communism is here to stay"—is the argument—"so let's recognize Red China." In the church we have adopted a similar policy of accommodation: "Let us accept things as they are and go along with the status quo. The end justifies the means." The Church at Corinth accepted the immorality of one of its members and was resigned to it. The church at Pergamos tolerated Balaamism, and Thyatira "suffered that woman Jezebel." Our Lord judges us in what we put up with as much as in what we actively practice. The minister therefore cannot resign himself to a situation when God wants him to change it or at least speak for God to the situation.

If the preacher is not to resign or become resigned, there is another thing he can do: *he can be re-signed.* Was it not a great preacher of the past who, in this discouragement, offered to resign only to receive from the Lord this impression: "What you need is not to resign your commission, but to have your commission resigned!"

Dr. C. I. Scofield tells us that in all the years he was associated with D. L. Moody, the great evangelist rarely prayed with him without asking God to renew Scofield's commission. "That petition always gave me food for thought, and sometimes anxious thought," he says. "Was it indeed true that I was going on in my ministry under an expired commission? Or, if matters were not at that sad pass, had the signature of my Master upon it grown dim?"

Dr. Scofield goes on: "In company with a good Welsh brother, I was once listening to a sermon on the healing of Naaman. It was a good sermon from a homiletical standpoint, and I admitted it to myself in a kind of protest against an inner feeling that somehow, good as it was, it was leaving me cold. Just then my friend leaned over and sighed, 'If only the dear brother would take a fresh dip in Jordan himself!' When the sermon was ended, *my* message had come from the Welsh brother. I walked away into the night, I know not whither, for death seemed in my heart, and I kept my face to the stars as I tried to tell God that I was the 'dear man' who needed that fresh dip in Jordan."

I used to think that it was only ministers who had fallen into grievous sin who needed a fresh dip in Jordan; but if I read my Bible aright, some of God's men had their commissions resigned in the midst of an active ministry. Joshua met the Captain of the Lord of Hosts when he was already the leader of his people. Isaiah had his lips touched with fire when he was already a prophet crying, "Woe is this!" and "Woe is that!"—he needed to get around to "Woe is me!" Daniel was man enough to turn down a king's table and spend a night in a lion's den rather than deny God; but he still needed an experience when his comeliness turned to corruption. Job had set an example of fortitude and faithfulness to God in the midst of unparalleled adversity; but he still needed to come to the day when he could say, "I have heard of thee by the hearing of the ear: but now mine eye seeth thee" (42:5). None of us begins to compare with these men even *before* they had their commissions resigned.

Many a minister needs such an experience when he is successful, prosperous, and popular, living in a whirl of activity with his church finances in good shape and himself among the top men in the synagogue. For all of that, the signature of God on his credentials may be growing dim. Leaving first love and then losing the joy of salvation may take place in the midst of what passes for a successful ministry. It is almost impossible to get at such a man and convince him of his plight. He may resent the suggestion. And if he should suspect his true condition, how and when can he be still long enough to get his commission resigned? There are substitutes: a post-graduate course (when he may already have more degrees than temperature!); a trip to Palestine; and ecclesiastical promotion. But these are only Abana and Pharpar, rivers of Damascus, when a man needs a fresh dip in Jordan.

D. L. Moody was in the midst of a most successful ministry when two old ladies kept praying that he might have a renewed commission—and he did! A book that helped me greatly at a turning-point in my life, *Deeper Experiences of Famous Christians*, is a long record of resigned credentials, men of God who came to a fresh dip in Jordan; and the amazing thing is that most of them were doing well, by ordinary standards, before their renewal. The average preacher today would be glad to settle for what most of them had *before* they moved out of their good into God's best.

One reason why we are satisfied with less these days is because most churches are. How many pulpit committees do you know who put first in their requirements for a new minister: "Does he know God? Is the Divine signature fresh upon him?" A lot of churches do not want a Jeremiah with the fire of God in his bones. He might make them too uncomfortable every Sunday!

Another angle does not even enter into our thinking any more. If a preacher should have a new experience with God, that does not necessarily mean that he would go up another rung on the ladder of success. In some quarters he might be demoted! It might mean loss of station, loss of honors, loss of friends. That is utterly foreign to our thinking these days when the positive thinkers are telling us that if we affirm our faith three times before breakfast, we shall be president of the company before we are forty. Plenty of congregations would not welcome the information if the pastor should have his commission renewed. In some situations, if a minister went all the way to his Lord without the camp bearing His reproach, it might be his last Sunday in that pulpit. A deeper experience of God is no guarantee of a call to a bigger church. A man had better not ask God to restamp his preaching orders these days with the idea that it will enhance his reputation and insure his succession. He had better be prepared to lose his reputation and forego his success, for "as the Master, so must the servant be." Never forget that John was on Patmos for "... *the word of God, and... the testimony of Jesus Christ...*" (Revelation 1:2). But, after all, Patmos was a promotion, for it gave us the Revelation!

One thing is certain: a minister may have his study walls lined with diplomas, his ordination papers signed by illustrious men, a sheaf of recommendations from the mighty of the land, but if the stamp of heaven on his commission is faint and fading, he had better close up shop and take time out until he can return to his pulpit with a brand-new autograph from God. When he is thus resigned, he will be reassigned, like Elijah, like Jonah, like Peter. He may be given the same task, for some churches need not a new preacher, but the same preacher renewed. Whatever the task, old or new, he is ready for anything because he is fresh from the Main Office. And he is equipped to serve out his earthly apprenticeship until that day when "his servants shall serve him: And they shall see his face; and his name shall be in their foreheads" (Revelation 22:3-4). That is the final and eternal autograph—and it will never fade!

CHAPTER 15

"... No Substitute for Victory"

But thanks be to God, which giveth us the victory through our Lord Jesus Christ (1 Corinthians 15:57).

For the first time in American history we fought, in Korea, a war which we did not call a war, although it took the lives of thousands of Americans. For the first time we fought a war without winning it. We celebrated the end of a war that never has ended and the beginning of a peace that never has begun. Since then the West has been both at war and at peace, a condition never known before. The old-timers were accustomed either to winning or losing, defeat or victory. That was before the "era of the Third Dimension" set in, the age of "Peace Without Victory."

We might have done something about all this in 1933 when, against the advice of some of our best leaders, we recognized anarchy as though it were decent government, conferred on gangsters the status of gentlemen, and welcomed into the family of nations a devilish conspiracy that should have been isolated and quarantined from the start. Communism is a cancer and you cannot coexist peacefully with cancer.

Something might have been done when communism began in China, but a lot of people called it only an "agrarian reform." What was then a tiny serpent became a boa constrictor crushing, in its own nest, one-fourth of the human race.

When General Douglas MacArthur was called home from Korea, he said something that will stay said: "In war, there is no substitute for victory." There is an alternative—defeat—but there is no substitute. Much of the wretchedness of this weird and uncanny hour is the fruit of a futile and impossible program of *peace without victory.*

I am an American and I love my country. I am a Christian and I love the church. A parallel situation exists in both today; the devil is using the same strategy in both cases. Communism has won more in a cold war than ever could have been won in a hot war; so has the devil. We are living in moral fogs and spiritual twilights, conditions of low visibility, "the climate of consent." Black and white have been smudged into indefinite gray. Our greatest peril is not the red nor the yellow nor the black, but rather the gray peril. We have become enamored of a third position which actually does not exist. We are experts in the art of almost saying something, with "a straightforward way of dodging the issue." Politicians run for something but there are no statesmen standing for something. Puppets have supplanted prophets and the trumpet gives an uncertain sound.

In the Word of God there is no substitute for victory. There is no middle ground. It is either, or; right, or wrong; saved, or lost; heaven, or hell. Its yea is yea and its nay nay. There is no place for a neither-nor third position. We are to be good soldiers of Jesus Christ, not belligerent but militant. If we do not win, we lose. There is no substitute for victory.

The tragedy of these times is that we stop short of victory. You will remember that the Israelites made peace with the inhabitants of Canaan instead of exterminating them as God had commanded. All the miseries of the Book of Judges may be traced to the mistakes recorded in the Book of Joshua. The Israelites made a futile attempt at peaceful coexistence; they got tired of fighting and settled for a truce instead of a triumph. It is the appalling error of Christians and churches today.

There is no substitute for victory over the world. Whosoever will be a friend of the world is the enemy of God. Worldly Christians are traitors. James calls them "adulterers" and "adulteresses." This is the age of flexibility in foreign policy in the state and in personal living in the church. It is a day of summit conferences and 38th Parallels. Our Lord did not work out an agreement with this world; He overcame it. We are not here to get along with it, but to overcome it as did our Lord. In evangelical Christianity, strange new doctrines of separation now flourish. What is taught is not separation at all, but peaceful coexistence. Under the guise of tolerance we have become chummy with a world that is no friend of grace to help us on to God. It is a vain attempt to live at peace without victory.

There is no substitute for victory over the flesh. Old Adam is not subject to the will of God. There is no peaceful coexistence in the seventh chapter of Romans. We cannot live at an armistice with our old natures; it is either defeat or victory. We are to put on the Lord Jesus Christ and make not provision for the flesh. Today we make amazing concessions to carnality. There is a flippancy toward evil and fools make a mockery of sin. We crack jokes about drunkenness and divorce. We turn tragedy into comedy. What some call "Christian tolerance" is really unchristian nonchalance. The flesh is not to be condoned, but crucified. There can be no peace with it; there must be victory over it.

There is no substitute for victory over the devil. Sometimes he goes about as a roaring lion—and you cannot talk things over with a lion! Sometimes he is disguised as an angel of light, creeping in so graciously that it seems almost unchristian to oppose him. The early Christians not only fought the good fight of faith, they fought for the faith. Paul did not believe in peaceful coexistence with unbelief. He said, in effect, "Let false teachers be damned!" The man who lambasts fundamentalists but never says a word about modernists—including the new varieties—will bear watching. Christians are sheep among wolves, but we must beware of wolves among the sheep. The shepherd who believes in that kind of peaceful coexistence is a hireling! Righteousness has no fellowship with unrighteousness. Light has no communion with darkness. Christ has no concord with Belial; it is "the impossible symphony." The believer has no part with an infidel. There can be no peaceful coexistence with evil.

Our Lord made peace through the blood of His cross. This generation wants Christ without the cross and will believe in Him if He will come down from the tree. Men are willing to accept the benefits of Calvary but are not willing to die with Him and rise to walk in newness of life. They want the privileges without the responsibilities, the promises without the commandments, the crown without the cross, peace without victory.

When we traffic with communism we give it status and respectability. When Christians do business with false doctrine, they equate it with truth, and the uninstructed man on the street sees no difference. When Christians do business with the world, they make worldliness respectable and give it the sanction of the church. When we do business with the flesh, we exalt what God says must be executed. When we do business with the devil, we give him recognition. There is no place for a summit conference with Satan. We are in a fight to the finish.

Are we soldiers or diplomats? We have never had more diplomats administering our foreign policy than during the past quarter of a century, and we have never lost more ground. Patrick Henry was not a diplomat. The colonists had tried diplomacy. The same situation prevails in the spiritual world. The sneaking, suave, subtle, satanic spirit of tolerance, appeasement, and compromise has brought us to terms with the world, a truce with the flesh, and an armistice with the devil.

> My soul, be on thy guard;
> Ten thousand foes arise;
> The hosts of sin are pressing hard
> To draw thee from the skies.
>
> Ne'er think the victory won,
> Nor lay thine armor down;
> The work of faith will not be done
> Till thou obtain the crown.

"Thanks be to God, which giveth us the victory through our Lord Jesus Christ" (1 Corinthians 15:57). That victory is purchased in the past, provided in the present, perfected in the future. There is no peace without it. There is no substitute for it.

CHAPTER 16

The Troubler From Tekoa

... I was no prophet, neither was I a prophet's son... And the Lord took me as I followed the flock, and the Lord said unto me, Go, prophesy unto my people Israel (Amos 7:14, 15).

Many years ago I attended a week of meetings in a small North Carolina mountain town. The preacher gave a message each morning from the Book of Amos. I had never heard anyone preach all week from one book of the Bible. It was expository preaching and it fascinated me. Moreover, it introduced me to Amos, the colorful country prophet who went up to Bethel and gave that religious and political center a brand of preaching they were not accustomed to hearing.

In later years, after a barren period in my own ministry, the Lord woke me up and led me into plain old-fashioned preaching. One of my first sermons was about Amos. I preached it almost everywhere I went. Homer Rodeheaver used to speak of it almost every time we were on the platform together. I believe he thought it was my best sermon. It became a sort of pattern for my preaching.

Amos was trained in none of the schools of men. He got his message from God as he meditated outdoors in his humble work. He said, "I was no prophet, neither was I a prophet's son; but I was an herdman, and a gatherer of sycomore fruit: And the Lord took me as I followed the flock, and the Lord said unto me, Go, prophesy unto my people Israel" (7:14-15). He was not a prophet by *profession:* "I was no prophet." He was not a prophet by *parentage:* "... neither was I a prophet's son"; his father had not made a preacher of him. He was a prophet by *providence:* "And the Lord took me...." What better credentials does any man need?

Amos was not angling for return engagements. He was a non-conformist, unregimented, unclassified. He had no sponsor but Almighty God. He was definitely "out of order" at Bethel; he should have made an appointment through the regular channels instead of simply walking into town and opening up unannounced. He would not likely be invited to many big churches today. He might be invited to leave town, but not to come to town.

When he was called to preach, Amos, like Paul, conferred not with flesh and blood. His orders were direct. No council of men validated his commission. It is doubtful whether he could have found one that would have approved him. (It would certainly be impossible today!) Nobody in the school of prophets would do that kind of preaching, so God picked an outsider who had never learned the trick of talking out of both sides of his mouth. Here was a plain countryman who knew no better than to say bluntly what others covered up by the alibi. Singlehanded, and with no promoter or "project," Amos was a lone voice in the wilderness of his day. Probably he was a little lean, a little hungry, and a little angry; indeed, Amos has been called "God's Angry Man." Amos had no "foundation" behind him, no expense account, and he had not even heard of Social Security! Like Elijah and John the Baptist, he was, under God, "on his own."

His theology came to him like Paul's in Arabia. His sermons were not slanted to avoid giving offense to the godless times in which he lived. He did not take the teeth out of his message in Tekoa or "gum it" at Bethel. He offended almost everybody, including Dr. Amaziah, the court preacher, who was horrified at this rustic nuisance. "Go back to the backwoods," he said, in effect; "you have no business on the boulevards. You are not good for national morale. This boorish preaching of wrath and judgment—have you never heard of the power of positive thinking?"

Amos had not learned that it is really not nice to name things. He did not generalize; he particularized. He began with the sins of other nations, the neighbors as it were, but he did not stop at the borders of Israel. He was not one who could denounce evil at a distance while seeing none close at hand. His bifocals took in both the far and the near.

It was an evil time and Amos called it just that. He could not have picked a time when his views would have seemed more out-of-step with the age. Business was booming. Everything was on the up-up-up. People never had it so good! Under Jeroboam II there was plenty of everything, including religion. Amos made light of that: "Come to Bethel, and transgress; at Gilgal multiply transgression..." (4:4). A country preacher speaking with such irony must have horrified the religious Bethelites, but within fifty years the judgment Amos prophesied came to pass.

Centuries later another preacher wrote, "... the days are evil" (Ephesians 5:16). This time it was a little Jew whose bodily presence, they said, was weak and his speech contemptible. If you had looked around at the grandeur and glory that was Rome, you might have said, "Paul, what do you mean? Look at this worldwide empire with its armies and art, its language and laws, its cities and culture. You should join the clubs and broaden your interests and widen your contacts. You are too provincial, too exclusive. And it is such poor psychology to say that the days are evil. Put on your rose-colored glasses and paint the clouds with sunshine! You will catch more flies with honey than with vinegar." But Paul was not in the fly-catching business. He looked like a nobody before Nero, but someone has said, "Now we call our dogs Nero and our boys Paul."

The days are evil now, what with abounding lawlessness and abating love. "When the Son of man cometh, shall he find faith on the earth?" (Luke 18:8). Perilous times are upon us and men will not endure sound doctrine. Our age bears all the characteristics of the days of Amos. People hated him for calling the days evil; Ahab despised Micaiah for prophesying evil concerning him, instead of good; and our Lord said the world hated Him because He testified of it that its works were evil. Plenty of sermons and magazine articles bewail the hour, and they say we need an Amos. But how far would Amos get in the First Church of any modern Bethel? Where is there a wilderness prophet now who will be quiet enough to get a message from God and brave enough to preach it?

All kinds of arguments are advanced against such preaching today. Some ask, "What good will it do?" That is not the test. Isaiah and Amos and our Lord Himself preached to God's people, but they refused the message. The prophet who tries to arouse the church today need not be surprised if he gets the same treatment. Amos did not change the situation, but he gave God's message to his generation and left it without excuse.

Such preaching will not build up a crowd, but the business of the prophet is to fill the pulpit, not the pews. Nowhere in the New Testament is the size of the crowd the criterion of good preaching. Our Lord sometimes preached His crowd away. It is not our business to make the message acceptable, but to make it available. We are not out to make them like it, but to see that they get it.

Ahab accused Elijah of troubling Israel. Elijah promptly set the matter straight: "I have not troubled Israel; but thou, and thy father's house, in that ye have forsaken the commandments of the Lord, and thou hast followed Baalim" (1 Kings 18:18). Elijah did not create the trouble; he revealed it. Amos belongs in the same category. We have a word for it nowadays—"troubleshooter." Big business employs men to look out for possible "bugs" and breakdowns, to locate and correct problems in the machinery. God calls such men in the church; they are New Testament prophets with an instinct for locating trouble and a genius for exposing it. Naturally they are not popular. It is much more pleasant to be a Gamaliel, keeping everything quiet in Jerusalem. Such men are called troublemakers, but they do not create the situation; they reveal it. They do not put delinquent Christians on the spot; such people are already on the spot. The prophet merely reveals the spot.

We need some sanctified troubleshooters today, for we have trouble aplenty. We are beset without and within. The atheists who hammer on the outside of the church make a lot of noise, but the pests who bore from within are doubly dangerous because they are so quiet about their work. Today the idea seems to have gotten around that we should never disturb the status quo, but should go along with it, termites and all. The church has a right and a duty to screen out all varieties of bugs.

Amos was a troubleshooter and yet there is a sense in which he was a troubler of Israel because he sought to arouse the conscience of the nation. A prophet is always disturbing; he is a cause of general uneasiness. He makes Ahab and Herod uneasy and keeps Darius awake all night. He plays havoc with the serenity school and irritates the tranquilizers. He has never learned to talk so that one half of what he says cancels the other half and he can finish without having said anything. Just when false prophets of peaceful coexistence have almost lulled everybody into a stupor, the true prophet blasts the neighborhood with a siren that cries aloud and spares not. He locates the trouble and proposes the remedy. He does not write a treatise on the subject; he calls to repentance. While scholars write wordy volumes that few people read, the prophet says it in one colorful paragraph. Joseph Parker said, "The man whose sermon is 'Repent' sets himself against his age and will for the time being be battered mercilessly by the age whose moral tone he challenges. There is but one end for such a man—'off with his head.' You had better not preach repentance until you have pledged your head to heaven."

It is not easy to be an Amos at Bethel, and the new polite little rules for successful preaching leave no room for such disturbers of the peace. No school can produce them and no school can stop them; they are odd numbers in a regimented day. May there be even now in the backwoods somewhere a solitary lad who will walk in prophetic succession to the "Troubler from Tekoa"!

CHAPTER 17

Pharisees or Christians?

For I say unto you, That except your righteousness shall exceed the righteousness of the scribes and Pharisees, ye shall in no case enter into the kingdom of heaven (Matthew 5:20).

When our Lord was upon earth His worst enemies were the Pharisees. Pharisaism shows up in several forms: in cold orthodoxy without the love of God; in religion that majors on the minors and minors on the majors, tithing of mint, anise, and cummin, while neglecting judgment, mercy, and faith; and in religious activity without the Spirit. This last is most dangerous of all because it is so deceptive.

There were many commendable things about the Pharisees. They studied the Scriptures, attended the house of God, prayed, tithed, lived separated lives, and sought to win others, compassing land and sea to make one proselyte. Yet Jesus said that the publicans and harlots would go into the Kingdom of God before them. A church full of Pharisees would be a remarkable institution. (I don't know of a church where all the members attend services, pray, study the Bible, tithe, live clean moral lives separated from the world, and seek to win others.) Yet a church filled with Pharisees would be a church filled with lost sinners and as sure for hell as a club of atheists. The Pharisees had no work of grace in their souls, no love of God in their hearts; they were strangers to the Holy Spirit.

Here is something very disturbing in our religious life today. All of these activities we have mentioned are the very things we are trying so hard to get our church members to do. Drives, contests, study courses, suppers, conventions, campaigns galore—all are aimed at getting church people to do what they should do anyway, and without all this pressure, because they love God. In fact, if they do these things for any reason other than love for Christ they might as well not do them at all, because only that activity which is the spontaneous expression of love for Him is acceptable in His sight. There is a frightening danger that we are developing Pharisees instead of growing Christians. It is possible to get a lot of people busy doing a lot of things Christians ought to do without their being Christians or having Christian motivation. We can build a religious empire, put up hundreds of church buildings, take in thousands of members, and raise millions of dollars by promotional methods under religious auspices—without the Holy Spirit being anywhere near the place.

All such exercises as going to church, giving, and witnessing for Christ are the natural, normal expressions of a healthy Christian. Study courses are not necessary to teach children to play; playing is the natural exercise of a healthy child. A sick child will not play, but we don't make him well by sending him out to play! Young people do not require promotional campaigns on how to fall in love; healthy young people naturally fall in love. We are trying to get disinterested church members to do what they don't want to do instead of developing healthy Christians who will do these things, not from artificial stimulation, but because to a Spirit-filled Christian it is doing what comes naturally.

Dr. Findley Edge wrote, "It is far easier to lead people to engage in action than it is to lead them to act from a Christian motivation. That is one reason it is so much easier to make Pharisees than it is to make Christians." He points out that in so doing we lead people to deceive themselves into thinking they are something they are not, thus "developing a massive number of 20th-century Pharisees." Certainly we aid in their self-deception and we bring down the judgment of God on ourselves as well as them.

One reason for this is that people are more interested in being religious than in being righteous: "The kingdom of God is not meat and drink; but righteousness, and peace, and joy in the Holy Ghost" (Romans 14:17). Plenty of people are interested in peace and joy but not in righteousness. They want to be happy but they do not want to get right, be right, live right. They are like a man with a broken arm, who says, "No, I do not want the arm set—I only want a shot to kill the pain." The business of a doctor is not to make people happy but to make them well. When they are well they will be happy. The gospel makes us right, then happy.

What did our Lord mean when He said, "... except your righteousness shall exceed the righteousness of the scribes and Pharisees, ye shall in no case enter into the kingdom of heaven"? How much better than a Pharisee can one be? Not much, religiously. But Jesus did not mean that we should add a few more activities. He meant another kind of righteousness: the imputed, imparted, implanted righteousness of Christ Himself who is made unto us righteousness. That is just what the Pharisees did not have.

The Pharisees were successors to Moses. Our Lord said, in effect, "Do as they say, not as they do" (Matthew 23:2-3). What they did was not the expression of the love of God in their hearts. The churches in Ephesus and Sardis did many good things, but their motivations and objectives were wrong. Why is one chapter in Matthew given to the denunciation of a group soon to go out of existence? Is there any relevance today? Yes, because we have more Pharisees than ever. I do not think that most of them intend to be Pharisees; they hardly suspect that they are, and would be dumbfounded to find it out. They may come to church, sing in the choir, teach in Sunday school, and support the church, but it is a performance and not an experience. Jesus called the Pharisees "hypocrites," which means "play-actors." They were pretending what was not real. This is a day of imitations. We have produced fruit and flowers that look so real as to deceive all but most careful observers. In the Parable of the Tares, the devil did not burn up the wheat or plow up the ground; he planted an *imitation.*

Our Lord said that if we abide in Him we shall produce much fruit. Trying to get church people to produce results without the cause, to abound in good works when they are not abiding in grace, produces an artificial Christianity that may deceive even religious experts but will never pass inspection at the bar of God. We need to get back to producing Christians instead of Pharisees, born-again disciples as well as believers whose activities are motivated by the Holy Spirit. True Christian activity is but the outliving of the inliving Christ. Without Him we can do nothing.

CHAPTER 18

The Counterfeit Millenium

Let no man deceive you by any means.... (2 Thessalonians 2:3).

Rip Van Winkle slept through a revolution. When he went to sleep, George III was ruler of America. When Rip awoke, George Washington was President of the United States. Rip did not know what had happened and started whooping it up for the king. He almost got into serious trouble—he was hollering for the wrong George!

In these tragic times many well-meaning but mistaken souls are making a similar mistake. They are not shouting for the former monarch of a past age as Rip Van Winkle did, but for the false messiah of an age to come.

In 2 Thessalonians 2, two personalities emerge at the end of the age: Christ and Antichrist. Christ will return one day to reign over a Kingdom of peace and plenty. But before He sets up His Kingdom, Antichrist will have his fling.

Satan is the Great Imitator. Every time God starts something, the devil comes up with a counterfeit. When Moses performs a miracle, Jannes and Jambres are on hand. So the Great Imitator presents a false millennium.

Many preliminary signs are offered from the new day promised by communism to the world brotherhood of religious liberals. By whatever name, this counterfeit millennium is the vain effort of old Adam to regain his lost Paradise and build the Kingdom without the King.

The spirit behind most of the movements now promising a new world is not Christian. It is not light breaking through but darkness settling down. It is unregenerate man trying to create a society that will exist only when Christ reigns.

115

The issue now, as ever, is Christ or Antichrist. It is either God who became Man or the man who will claim to be God. When our Lord came to earth there was a Roman peace—law and order by imperial force. Before He comes again there will be another Roman peace. That peace will be shattered when the true nature of Antichrist becomes apparent; but he will first delude mankind with his program.

We are seeing some advance notices even now. The blueprint for the last empire of the Caesars is foreshadowed in the confederation of Western Europe; NATO and other developments are straws in the wind. Ecumenical movements, overtures from Rome, the United Nations, and internationalism—all point toward the world church and the world state, the harlot and the beast. Regimentation, uniformity, and conformity, the leveling of the human race into one faceless mass—all are previews of the profane paradise when the counterfeit messiah shall reign.

The Fatherhood of God and brotherhood of man now promoted by unregenerate men is not the program of Christ but that of Antichrist. It is so cleverly designed that it appears unchristian to oppose it. The few who can distinguish truth from error these days are in for plenty of trouble. Important clergymen will endorse the false millennium. Churches will put it in their budgets. Idealists will crusade for it, supposing they are "bringing in the Kingdom." It will offer rash amateurs and misguided youths a cause and a chance to be martyrs. It will provide a field day for all Rip Van Winkles who suddenly wake up and must "holler," even though it be "for the wrong George."

The history of human depravity began when men "changed the truth of God into a lie..." (Romans 1:25). It will reach its climax when "God shall send them strong delusion, that they should believe a lie" (2 Thessalonians 2:11). The devil is a liar and the father of the lie (John 8:44). He began his deception in the Garden of Eden when he told Eve: "Ye shall not surely die" (Genesis 3:4). All the unmentionable sins of Romans 1 grew out of that initial deception.

Before our Lord returns, many will come saying, "I am Christ," and they shall deceive many. That deception will reach its consummation in the ultimate lie, the man of sin—Antichrist.

We are being primed today for that final delusion. P. T. Barnum, the showman, said, "The American people love to be humbugged." We take to it like ducks to water. This is the most sophisticated and, at the same time, the most gullible generation in history. We buy more gold bricks and white elephants than all our forefathers. Throughout the day and most of the night we are barraged over radio and television by singing commercials: "This is the best detergent, the best automobile, the best anything, and everything. *It* has the new secret ingredient that nothing else has!" We know it is hokum, but we buy it just the same. In a thousand subtle ways we are being brainwashed for the ultimate lie.

While riding on a bus recently, I heard two men discussing the times and proposing their cures for the world's predicament. It was the same story, old Adam trying to produce world peace without Christ. I said to myself, "Two more candidates for the devil's millennium!" We hear it in panel, forum, and symposium, where, as one writer puts it, "We pool our ignorance." By education, sanitation, legislation, we are going to bring in the new earth.

Better environment is not enough. Adam was in Paradise when he fell! If better conditions were the answer, Adam would never have sinned. We've never had it as good since.

Mixing everybody into one Mulligan stew won't do it, either. There are a lot of bad eggs in humanity, but we are not going to improve them by scrambling them into one big omelet.

Christians should work with others, of course, in maintaining law and order, in seeking as much peace as is possible under the circumstances. But we must do it realizing that all such measures are only temporary. We will not pay *any* price for peace nor be snared into unholy alliances with this age by the argument that the end justifies the means.

We do not expect old Adam to regain Paradise. Spurgeon said, "Apart from the second coming of Christ, the world is more likely to sink into a pandemonium than to rise to a millennium. We are not building the Kingdom now. Our time is coming. Our King will set up the Kingdom when He comes. In this age it is a spiritual kingdom in the hearts of men, not meat and drink but righteousness, peace and joy in the Holy Ghost."

Satan will launch modern movements under religious auspices in order to maneuver Christians into an awkward position. But we must not be taken in by advance agents of a counterfeit millennium. One of these days, many well-meaning church people will wake up to find out that they have been looking toward and working for, not the Kingdom of God, but the devil's paradise. All true believers will have been caught up before that awful deception is fully revealed. In the meantime, let us busy ourselves with our Saviour's program until He comes.

The principles of the Kingdom of God cannot be woven by unregenerated men into the pattern of our pagan society. The blueprints of the age to come cannot be forced upon this present world. The Sermon on the Mount cannot be legislated into the constitutions of this earth. Today false messiahs cry, "Lo, here!" and "Lo, there!" announcing false kingdoms and counterfeit millenniums. No matter how much Scripture may be quoted or how many prominent churchmen endorse such projects, Christians who support them are "hollering for the wrong George."

Lenin said to his Bolsheviks: "We will find our most fertile field for infiltration of Marxism within the field of religion, because religious people are the most gullible and will accept almost anything if it is couched in religious terminology."

The church missed the road centuries ago when Christians ceased being pilgrims and strangers in an unfriendly world; instead of looking for their King to return, they began building the Kingdom down here. Since then they have been hooked into all kinds of projects and taken for a ride on all kinds of bandwagons. These movements, not of God, bring only disappointment, for, as Bishop Ryle has said, "Nothing so chills and dampens the faith of Christians as indulgence in unscriptural expectations."

Dr. Thomas F. Torrance of Edinburgh has said that "in due time even so-called Christian organizations may easily reveal themselves as a part of a many-headed monster of evil, the more monstrous because it is worldwide and bears Christian similitude." We must not be tricked by advance agents of Antichrist into becoming a part of the gigantic program of the last days that would deceive the very elect.

Our Lord delivered no lectures on how much tax to pay to Caesar, and Paul held no seminars on slavery. Let the church regain her peculiar and distinctive message. It is not her duty to beat the drums and second the motion for any project of this world nor to become a party to any crusade promoting a false millennium.

One is reminded of the would-be cellist who kept sawing away on one note. Somebody said to him, "That is not the way to play. You should not keep your finger on one string, but run up and down the strings." He objected, "Those fellows are looking for the right note, but I've found it!" The church has the right note for this or any other day, and Christians have no business playing any of the tunes of this age.

It may seem monotonous to keep on preaching the gospel when men want to strike another pitch more in keeping with the mood of this generation. It is grim tragedy when good people become so confused as to mistake the tricks of Antichrist for the work of God. The sin against the Holy Spirit in the days of our Lord lay in ascribing the work of God to the devil. It begins to look as though this generation might reverse the process and ascribe the work of the devil to God. Antichrist conducts a twofold campaign today: it is destructive in crime, war, the breakdown of our homes, in physical, mental, and moral degradation; but it is also deceptive in false movements that promise peace and brotherhood. One part of the crusade is negative, the other positive. The positive is more dangerous than the negative because many good people are misled by false projects under religious auspices. Satan does more harm as an angel of light than as a roaring lion. As frightening as present-day lawlessness and moral rottenness may be, greater is the danger from the paradise he promises than from the pandemonium he produces.

Dr. Harry A. Ironside wrote that the rider on the white horse in Revelation 6 is "man's last effort to bring in a reign of order and peace while Christ is still rejected, the devil's cunning scheme for bringing in a false millennium without Christ." Dr. Torrance calls the 666 of Revelation 13:18 "the number of so-called Christian civilizations without Jesus Christ." All the efforts of unregenerate men to build an ideal world fall short of perfection, as 666 falls short of 777. The only complete solution of earth's troubles lies in our Lord's return, and in the meantime any true betterment of society is the fruit of the gospel even as the Wesleyan revival saved England and started a flow of social and national blessings that bear fruit to this day.

Babel was man's effort at unity, and God cursed it with tongues no one could understand. Pentecost was God's plan of unity, and He blessed it with tongues everyone could understand. This age is witnessing another Babel of man's devising. It is not the business of the church to sponsor and bless such towers toward heaven. We must not confuse the coming Kingdom with the counterfeit. This is no time to be "hollering for the wrong George."

Rip Van Winkle was confused because he had been asleep. "It is high time to awake out of sleep: for now is our salvation nearer than when we believed" (Romans 13:11).

The wide-awake Christian is not deceived. He reads between the lines and interprets what he reads in the light of the Bible, not the news commentators. Dr. Mordecai Ham used to say, "I read the newspapers to find out what man is doing; then I read the Bible and find out what God is going to do." The Christian is not swept off his feet by popular movements of unregenerate men to create heaven on earth. He renders unto Caesar the things which are Caesar's, but he will not give to Caesar what belongs to God. He does not think the choice today is between being Red or dead—which reminds us of the Israelites when they murmured, "It is better to serve the Egyptians than to die in the wilderness."

The pressure on the Christian, however, will be terrific. The subtle, suave, satanic brainwashing from the world of Antichrist will beset him day and night. He will be ostracized, called unchristian and unloving because he does not endorse the advance programs that prepare for the coming worship of the beast. He will not confuse the rider of the white horse in Revelation 6 with the Rider in Revelation 19.

Moreover, he will be embarrassed by prophecy faddists who cast reproach on the real truth by wild perversions. But his will be the blessing promised to all who read and hear and keep the message of the Apocalypse. Well did Godet write, "The more deeply the church plants in the earth the stakes of her tent and establishes herself at her ease here below, the more does the Apocalypse become to her a foreign and even repulsive book. The more, on the other hand, tempestuous winds shake the curtains of her temporary dwelling place and threaten to break their cords, the more does she feel the value of this marvelous book which teaches her to look up continually toward the Bridegroom Whose return she expects."

The wise Christian wastes no time trying to explain God's program to unregenerate men; it would be casting pearls before swine. He might as well try to describe a sunset to a blind man or discuss nuclear physics with a monument in a city park. The natural man cannot receive such things. One might as well try to catch sunbeams with a fishhook as to lay hold of God's revelation unassisted by the Holy Spirit. Unless one is born of the Spirit and taught by Him, all this is utterly foreign to him. Being a Ph.D. does not help, for in this realm it could mean "Phenomenal Dud"!

A man on trial was told by the judge: "You may choose a lawyer. There is one over there to your right, another to your left, and another out in the hall." The man looked to the lawyers right and left and said, "Judge, I'll take a chance on the one in the hall." Today the Christian is looking neither to the right nor left. His Advocate, the Saviour, is in the hall, "even at the door." But there is another also in the hall: the grim figure of Antichrist looms without. When he first appears he will not seem grim but gracious. His advance stooges are already with us, so pleasant as to make it appear evil not to endorse them. "False Christs and false prophets shall rise, and shall shew signs and wonders, to seduce, if it were possible, even the elect. *But take ye heed:* behold, I have foretold you all things" (Mark 13:22-23).

CHAPTER 19

"... Nothing to Set Before Him"

... I have nothing to set before him... (Luke 11:6).

The gospel of Luke records what I like to call the Parable of the Three Friends. They were the friend who came in his journey and found no food, the friend who had no bread for his guest, and the friend who supplied the need.

This is a very disturbing story. Everybody in it was disturbed: the visitor who found nothing to eat must have been embarrassed; his host who had no bread was mortified; the friend aroused at midnight had his rest interrupted and his sleep broken. It was a very disturbing evening and its applications ought to disturb us.

The first of these friends was *a friend to feed:* "A friend of mine in his journey is come to me..." (Luke 11:6). All of us have such friends. Parents may well reflect that their children are in a very real sense their friends who have come to them in their journeys, and they must be fed—body, mind, and spirit. Sunday school teachers should never forget that their classes are made up of friends on journeys. Certainly all ministers should see their congregations as a host of friends come in their journeys—and how hungry!

Woe to the preacher who gets accustomed to facing needy hearts and starving souls on Sunday morning! There is enough drama packed in any Sunday congregation to fill a shelf of books. What headaches and heartaches are hidden in Sunday clothes! Like King Jehoram, they wear royal robes without, but sackcloth next to their flesh. For all one knows, that man on the right may be on the verge of suicide. That family on the center aisle may break up next week. That girl on the left may have a ruined life by next Sunday. That businessman may be in his grave. These are our friends who have come to us in their journeys and it is up to us to feed them.

Our Lord said of the hungry multitude on one occasion, "They need not depart; give ye them to eat" (Matthew 14:16). This poor hungry world never needs to leave Jesus; it need not go into communism, it need not depart into crime and shame, it need not resort to the pleasures of sin to satisfy its hunger. "They need not depart; give ye them to eat." Our friends have come in their journeys and we ought to get the food out. God forbid that we should give stones for bread, serpents for fish, scorpions for eggs! Some pulpits serve just that—stones, serpents, scorpions!

Then there was *a friend in need:* "I have nothing to set before him" (Luke 11:6). That is the plight of every preacher on Sunday morning if left to himself—and the sooner he finds it out, the better! It is the Word of God that feeds our souls, and not our remarks. We must not confuse the dishes with the food. Suppose you were invited to a home for dinner. You sat down at the appointed place and time. The silver, the crystal, everything was in order. Somebody returned thanks—but there was no food! That is a perfect description of some church services.

We preachers should improve our diction, brush up on our grammar, enlarge our vocabularies, but the bread comes down from heaven. We cannot depend on a deep freeze of old sermons or some fancy recipe we have made up. The best we can serve up is only a sprig of parsley, and it is only the garnish. What feeds the souls of men is not our trimmings but God's truth. Some sermons are all garnish with not enough meat and potatoes to feed one soul for one day. The sooner we learn that we have nothing to set before our friends who have come to us in their journeys, the better it will be for us and for our friends. If we do not know how to pray down bread from heaven we shall be pulpit Mother Hubbards whose cupboards are bare.

The third friend in Luke's parable was *a friend in deed.* The *friend in need* with *a friend to feed* found his way to the house of the *friend in deed.* Actually the emphasis here is not on importunity, although the story has gotten that reputation. The lesson is not in similarity but in contrast. The key is in verse 13: "If ye then, being evil, know how to give good gifts unto your children: *how much more* shall your heavenly Father give the Holy Spirit to them that ask him?" The word "importunity" in this parable carries the idea of shamelessness. The *friend in need* created a commotion, alarmed the neighborhood, set the dogs to barking; he was persistent, insistent. We have a right to come boldly to the throne of grace and approach with confidence the door of heaven, for it is our Father's house.

It comes to this: the preacher who has bread to set before his friends on their journeys is the preacher who knows how to pray. "What a preacher is in his prayer closet is what he is"—it is the true measure of the man. "We can do more than pray after we have prayed, but we cannot do more than pray until we have prayed." We are never taller than when we are on our knees.

John G. Paton's father curtained off a corner of his little home in Scotland for a place to pray. The children learned to tiptoe past that sacred spot. The preacher who has not learned to curtain off a big corner of his time to stock up on bread from heaven is headed for catastrophe.

> There is a viewless cloistered room
> As high as heaven, as fair as day,
> Where, though my feet may join the throng,
> My soul can enter in and pray.
> One hearkening even cannot know
> When I have crossed the threshold o'er,
> For He alone who hears my prayer
> Has heard the shutting of the door.

We do not always pray best in some favored quiet spot. How blessed to know that in the tumult of home or shop or office, or on the crowded street, we can close our eyes for a moment and be instantly in another world! It is no farther than that to the Father's house!

When Absalom was slain, Ahimaaz had no tidings ready but reported only a tumult. Some preachers are in a similar predicament because they get their sermons up instead of down. We must *come* to the Father's house and *commune* with the Father in prayer before we *communicate* for the Father from the pulpit.

We marvel at lives such as that of David Brainerd. Perhaps the secret lies in these words of his: "I prayed privately with a dear friend and I think I scarce ever launched so far into the eternal world as then. I got so far out in the broad ocean that my soul with joy triumphed over all the evils on the shores of mortality. I think that time and all its gay amusements and cruel disappointments never appeared so inconsiderable to me before." Here was an astronaut who got clear to heaven on wings of prayer. Most of us never do more than fly a kite now and then. There is as much difference between exploring the world of prayer and merely talking about it as there is between a world traveler and a clerk in a travel office. There is just as much room in the world of spirit as in the world of space. Prayer has four boundaries: according to His Word, according to His will, according to our need, according to our faith. No man need feel restricted with that much latitude!

We have friends to feed and we are friends in need because we do not pray to the Friend in Deed. We discuss ways and means, we ponder the status quo, and all the while our Lord stands in our little committee rooms, asking, "Why reason ye among yourselves, because ye have brought no bread?" (Matthew 16:8). But it is not enough to have bread for our friends; That bread must be distributed in the power of the Spirit. So we read, "How much more shall your heavenly Father give *the Holy Spirit* to them that ask him?"

We go to the Father's house not only for provision, but for power. It is not enough to preach the Bible; it must be preached in the same power that inspired it. God grant to us His bread and His blessing!

Chapter 20

F-a-i-t-h

... According to your faith be it unto you (Matthew 9:29).

Some time ago, while checking my concordance on the word "all," I was impressed with what might be called *the "allness" of our sinfulness:* "*All* have sinned, and come short of the glory of God" (Romans 3:23); "The scripture hath concluded *all* under sin..." (Galatians 3:22); "For whosoever shall keep the whole law, and yet offend in one point, he is guilty of *all* (James 2:10); "Except ye repent, ye shall *all* likewise perish" (Luke 13:3).

We are *all* sinners. We do not have to break all the commandments to be involved; and unless we repent we shall all perish. This does not mean that one man is as vile morally as another, or that one is as great a menace to society as another; but it does mean that all of us are sinners. Nicodemus was as truly a sinner as Barabbas, though not to the same degree.

I was impressed, however, with something more: *the "allness" of our Saviour:* "Christ is *all,* and in *all*" (Colossians 3:11); He "filleth *all* in *all*" (Ephesians 1:23); He "is before *all* things, and by him *all* things consist"; "For in him dwelleth *all* the fulness of the Godhead bodily"; in Him "are hid *all* the treasures of wisdom and knowledge" (Colossians 1:17; 2:9; 2:3). The answer to the allness of my sin is the "allness" of my Saviour. The way from the one to the other is by faith.

Someone has said that the letters in the word "faith" may be spelled out to mean "For all, I take Him." True faith in Christ means, first, that for all He is and all He claimed to be—Son of God, Saviour of the world—I take Him. God has taken care of everything in Jesus Christ; He is the answer to every question in time and eternity. "He that spared not his own Son, but delivered him up for us *all*, how shall he not with him also freely give us *all* things?" (Romans 8:32).

We may also spell "faith" to mean "Forsaking all, I take Him." I must forsake my sins (Proverbs 28:13); forsaking my sins, I take Him as Saviour; then I must forsake *all* that I have (Matthew 19:27-29; Luke 14:33). This does not mean I am to walk out of my home, leaving family and friends; it means that He must come first. Better still, my love and loyalty to Him includes and glorifies all other loves and loyalties. Forsaking *all* I have, I take Him as my Lord.

We may also spell "faith" to mean "For all, I trust Him." I trust Him for all my *need:* "My God shall supply *all* your need according to his riches in glory by Christ Jesus (Philippians 4:19). He is able to make *all* grace abound toward us, that we always, having *all* sufficiency in *all* things, may abound to every good work (2 Corinthians 9:8). We are to cast *all* our care upon Him, and we can do *all* things through Him (1 Peter 5:7; Philippians 4:13). My past, my present, my future—for everything I need, I trust Him.

Finally, we may spell "faith" to mean "For *all*, I thank Him": for what He has done, is doing, will do. "In every thing give thanks..." (1 Thessalonians 5:18). For everything? Yes, because *all* things work together for our good if we love God and are the called according to His purpose. We are to make our requests known with thanksgiving, and God's peace will garrison our hearts and minds (Philippians 4:6).

For *all*, I take Him; for *all*, I trust Him; for *all*, I thank Him— here is a formula that never fails. I have indicated only a few of the Scriptures that mark out this blessed path to peace and power. Accept it, affirm it, act upon it—not as a magic "open sesame," but as God's Word—and you will find that through appropriating faith the *allness* of His grace is the answer to the *allness* of your need.

CHAPTER 21

Living in Nazareth

And he did not many mighty works there because of their unbelief (Matthew 13:58).

Our Lord did not have a very successful meeting with the hometown folks in Nazareth. The three elements necessary to a good meeting were present: "Where two or three are gathered together in my name"—the *place;* "there am I"—the *Person;* "in the midst of them"—the *people* (Matthew 18:20). At Nazareth "he [the *Person*] did not many mighty works there [the *place*] because of their unbelief [the *people*]" (Matthew 13:58). The trouble lay with the people. What form did their unbelief take?

Our Lord was a *Prophet* without honor in His own country. The Nazarenes could not accept Him as the Son of God. They were astonished and credited Him with mighty works, but He had not been to the schools of the rabbis. To this day there are those who will not accept any prophet who does not fit into their plans and specifications; if he has not been to the schools, everything he does and says is discounted. Hopelessly blinded by their provincialism, they view the prophet with complacency, if not with contempt, from the lofty heights of their intellectual stratosphere.

It was familiarity that lay behind the Nazarene unbelief. Jesus was just one of the local boys. The townspeople knew His family and they had known Him for years. They knew Him—*and they didn't know him!*

It is possible in more ways than one to live in Nazareth today so that our Lord can do no mighty works among us because of our unbelief. One may know much about Jesus without really knowing Him at all. The Nazarenes were too close to Him; their very advantage became a disadvantage. They were so close to Him that they were far from Him. So, too, may we draw nigh to Him with our mouths and honor Him with our lips while our hearts are far from Him.

I lived for years in a historic old city. People came from afar to see its sights. I lived almost next door to all of it and missed most of it. So may we live in the midst of spiritual realities without knowing them in experience. It is a wonderful thing to grow up in a Christian home, but it can also be very dangerous. As a boy I was saturated with Bible truth. I read through the New Testament again and again, was licensed to preach at eleven years of age, and ordained when I was fifteen. I wrote sermons for the local newspaper before I reached my teens, preached regularly when I was twelve. But there came a day when I had to put myself in a corner and ask myself, "Is all of this real to you, or is it merely patter you have learned to recite like a parrot?" It has been said that nothing is more perilous to a real Christian experience than a superficial knowledge of the language of Christianity from childhood.

I read of a man who had learned to read Arabic with ease, but could not speak enough Arabic to order a cup of coffee. So may the things of God become the vernacular of the mind but never the speech of the heart. It is possible to be a walking encyclopedia of Bible information, knowing "all the answers" without knowing Him who is the Answer. God's Word is a light and a lamp, but we are to walk in that light, not merely stare at it. There is such a thing as being blinded by an excess of light. The very light that brightens our path will blind us if we misuse it.

When our Lord was on earth, the people we would have expected to know Him best—the Pharisees, the Nazarenes, the rich ruler—never really knew Him. But Bartimaeus, Zacchaeus, the Syrophoenician woman, plain fishermen—they knew Him best. The Nazarenes knew too much and did not know enough. I remember a sign in an old country doctor's office: "It's what you learn after you know it all that counts!" It is possible to sit in a library of books about Jesus, to be busy seven days a week in Christian work, and all the while to be like a cat drowning in cream. We can know too little because we know too much.

One thinks of the old hillbilly who had lived almost all his days in a cabin facing a towering mountain. He had never climbed it. Eventually a road was built clear to the top and a friend took him up the winding curves until he stood on the summit with a breathtaking view before him in all directions. The tears coursed down his weather-beaten face and he murmured, "Just think, I've lived here all my life in reach of this, and almost missed it!" So may one live in proximity to the truth, as near to the Lord as the Nazarenes to Jesus, and never behold what God has prepared for those who love Him.

When I started out in a traveling ministry I had the idea that being in good meetings all the time would carry me along on its own momentum. Nothing can be more devastating to a deep Christian experience than being in the midst of religious activity all the time. We sink into a sort of stupefaction. We know all about it but we see few miracles. We become professionals "trafficking in unfelt truth."

Someone has said, "I wish I could read the Gospel of John for the first time." I know what he meant; he had gotten used to it. Leaving first love and then losing the joy of salvation is not the exclusive experience of backsliders who have quit reading the Bible and going to church. One may be busy with the things of God and all the while be getting farther away from experiencing the very truths he labors to perpetuate.

It was said of the Greek church scholars of the tenth century: "They held in their lifeless hands the riches of their fathers without inheriting the Spirit which had created and improved that sacred patrimony. They read, they praised, they compiled, but their languid souls seemed alike incapable of thought and action." So may we handle the coinage of God's truth without ever examining it for ourselves to know whose image and superscription may be thereupon.

How can old truths be made to glow with new meaning? When one visits historic spots he needs a guide. Places loaded with significance will be passed by if there is no one to explain their importance. The facts about Christ, the truths of God's Word take on life and warmth and meaning when the Holy Spirit is our Interpreter. John Wesley was an Oxford scholar and a religious man, but it was not until the Spirit set his heart ablaze that England caught fire. Like Job, Wesley had heard with the hearing of the ear, but then he saw.

Do you know Jesus Christ in a conscious, compelling, continuing, challenging experience, or do you live in Nazareth, a next-door neighbor to the Lord but ignorant of His miracle-working power because of your unbelief? One may work in a travel office, sell tickets, and hand out folders about foreign lands without ever leaving the old hometown. It takes more than a suitcase covered with foreign labels to make a world traveler. One can make a living handling the things of God with no firsthand knowledge of any of them. One may make a business of starting other people toward the Promised Land without ever leaving Egypt.

Here is the test of every church meeting: we may have the Person, the place, and the people, but can our Lord do a mighty work or will He be hindered by our unbelief? I do not mean the unbelief of the agnostic or the worldling, the outsider we call a sinner. I mean the unbelief of Nazareth, of church people, of religious workers who sing and speak the Saviour's name but who suffer from a deadly unbelief. It is possible to be guilty of *unbelieving belief*, to have real faith in Christ but to give way at times to doubt. It is infinitely worse to be guilty of *believing unbelief* that accepts the facts about Him but never really knows Him, He Himself declared that one may prophesy in His name, cast out demons, and do wonderful works, and still hear Him say at that great day, "I never knew you..." (Matthew 7:23).

You must be nearer to Jesus than a fellow-citizen of Nazareth. It is not enough to be His next-door neighbor in the old hometown.

Chapter 22

No Home Down Here

For I am now ready to be offered, and the time of my departure is at hand. I have fought a good fight, I have finished my course, I have kept the faith (2 Timothy 4:6-7).

By now some of us are beginning to rate as old-timers. We can remember when "I Am Bound for the Promised Land" was almost a theme song of the saints. "In the Sweet By-and-By" and "When I Can Read My Title Clear" were cut from the same piece. We took seriously the Scriptures' reminder that this world is not our rest, that we are strangers and pilgrims seeking a city. We were in full agreement with what Dr. G. Campbell Morgan's biographer says of the great expositor's father: "He lived with a Bible in his hand and his face toward a better world."

Any man who believes his Bible will live that way. Say what you will, the Old Book gives no comfort to those who would drive down their tent pegs in these lowlands. It warns against the love of money, the cares of this life, and the pride of it. It would have us love not the world but lay up our treasure in heaven. It reminds us that a man's life consisteth not in the abundance of the things which he possesseth. It admonishes us to be content with food and raiment, and such things as we have.

It is high time we heeded such counsel. We used to feel like traveling on; now we feel like settling down. This wonderland of plastics and gadgets, deep freezes and give-away shows, ranch houses in Suburbia and push-button living, seems good enough for most of the saints.

Of course, God's people have a right to the common comforts of life. There is no holiness in a hair shirt. The old mystics were sometimes mistaken; we are pilgrims, not hermits, and living in a hole does not make us any holier. On the other hand, the new fad for equating Christianity with earthly prosperity is hard put to it to find New Testament texts for its position. Our Lord had nowhere to lay His head; He was not at home down here. The early saints bear little resemblance to the new variety, who are not out to overcome the world, but to enjoy it. The heroes of faith in Hebrews 11 do not remind us of many modern "successful Christians." And what shall we say of Paul, who said that the apostles were made as the world's rubbish, the scum of the earth?

Many times, while visiting in some lovely mountain retreat or palatial house by the lake, I have thought to myself: "What a book I could write if I lived here!" Then I have had better second thoughts and remembered that the New Testament was not written on vacation. Much of it was penned in jail! Paul was not in a pleasure resort when he gave us the Epistles. John Bunyan did not turn out *Pilgrim's Progress* from a villa on the Riviera.

We are plainly bidden in Scripture not to be conformed to the world. We seem to have forgotten the admonition. The inspiration of most Christians today is not the faithful, cross-bearing disciple but the successful big-shot. We use the same standards this world uses, except that we glorify them with our religious phraseology.

There is no denying it: the tenor of the New Testament and the spirit of the early Christians are foreign to our present-day at-homeness in this world. That spirit prevailed until Constantine paganized Christianity by trying to Christianize paganism. Then we lost our pilgrim character and the marks of our heavenly citizenship. The church ceased to look for the Lord from heaven; she settled down like Lot in Sodom, and became a gigantic supercorporation, another big business, so like the age in which she lives that few can see the difference. It was a dark day when the church forgot that we have no home down here.

Christianity always makes a new start when some faithful remnant, despised by the world, a speckled bird in the eyes of conventional Christianity, produces a new band of pilgrims bound for the Promised Land. A religious leader spoke recently about the danger of becoming a "church" instead of a "sect." He said that a "sect" is usually small and poor and rises up against the sins and evils of its day, whereas a "church" moves out on Front Street, its membership made up of the so-called best people, and conforms to a self-centered, complacent society.

It is possible to have a big bank account and be poor in spirit, but the combination is rare. Smyrna piety is not often mixed with Laodicean prosperity. When we are rich and increased with goods we usually have need of nothing. If we can use the world without abusing it, well and good; but when we feather the nest too well the eaglets do not fly.

Going to heaven does not thrill the saints much today. It has been a long time since I have heard an old-fashioned sermon about heaven. "There's a land that is fairer than day," but most of us are not looking that far; we are nearsighted. No longer do we view the distant scene; we are satisfied to watch the nearest TV screen. At best, we think of ourselves as citizens of earth trying to get to heaven, when really we are citizens of heaven sojourning on earth.

There can be no question about it—we are finding this world more attractive than did our forbears. Bunyan's Christian had no use for Vanity Fair; nowadays we have come to terms with it. We enjoy some, if not all, of it; at best we are out to reform it, not escape it. But the old "mammy" who said, "I wears dis world lak a loose garment" had the right idea. She would not be wrapped in the trappings of this age.

Dr. J. B. Phillips says of the early Christians: "To these men this world was only a part, and because of the cumulative result of human sin, a highly infected and infectious part of God's vast universe, seen and unseen. They trained themselves therefore, and attempted to train others not to be 'taken in' by this world nor give their hearts to it, not to conform to its values, but to remember constantly that they were only temporary residents, and that their rights of citizenship were in the unseen world of Reality. As we read what they have to say, we may perhaps find ourselves saying a little wistfully, 'perhaps these men were right.'"

Christianity always loses ground when Christians make themselves at home down here. We are spiritual children of Abraham, not sons of Lot. The moment we settle down, we cease to be pilgrims. Then we change our theology to suit our practice. We decide to build the Kingdom here instead of bringing back the King. We forget that the Holy City comes down and that the present order is doomed to destruction no matter how we dress it up. What use is it to set our affections upon it or lay up treasure in it? We but gather spoil for moths and thieves. We have no certain dwelling place down here.

Several Bible characters warn us of this folly. Consider Baruch, the secretary of Jeremiah. He had a spell of the blues and God said to him, "Seekest thou great things for thyself? seek them not" (Jeremiah 45:5). In other words, "This is no place to feather your nest. You have no home down here." In the New Testament there was Demas who forsook Paul, "having loved this present world" (2 Timothy 4:10). I do not know what triggered his decision or what form his defection took, but Demas liked it too well down here. He may have ended up as mayor of a town, with plenty of stocks and bonds. When Paul ended his career he had no stocks save those on his feet, and no bonds except those on his wrists. But today Paul is our inspiration and Demas is only a warning.

I must confess that through the years I have had difficulty harmonizing our standards of success in the ministry with the Bible picture of the rough road the prophets trod. My New Testament tells me about the way of a cross, reproach, persecution, and suffering. When I listen to the shop-talk in religious gatherings, when I watch the scramble for top seats in the synagogue, when I behold the wire-pulling and politicking for posh pastorates, I cannot make the modern tune fit the Bible words.

I have read somewhere of a wild duck on migration that came down into a barnyard where tame ducks were feeding. He liked the food so well that he stayed a day, a week, a month, then the whole season. One day he heard a familiar honking high overhead and he recognized the call of his erstwhile companions winging their way home. His eyes sparkled, his heart beat faster, and he rose to join them. But, alas, he had fed too well and could get no higher than the eaves of the barn! The story goes that he said to himself, "Oh, well, what difference does it make? I like it here." So he spent the rest of his life in a barnyard. The day came when his old companions passed over and he never even heard their call.

I have seen men and women who once mounted up with wings as eagles but who are now content to live in the barnyard of this world. Sometimes, in an old-fashioned meeting under the spell of powerful preaching, they catch a few notes of the life they used to know, "the song of saints on higher ground." Their hearts may beat a little faster and their eyes may fill with tears. There may even be a momentary impulse to sing:

> My heart has no desire to stay
> Where doubts arise and fears dismay.

But, alas, they have fed too well on the fleshpots of Egypt! They like it too well down here, and finally they reach that sad state where they no longer respond to the call from on high.

I beg you, do not settle down in the barnyard of this world. We Christians have no continuing city, but we seek one to come. We have no home down here.

CHAPTER 23

In Times Like These

... wait on the Lord, and he shall save thee (Proverbs 20:22).

If one wants to know what time it is by God's clock and what His program is for these frightening times, he will find out not by listening to experts, but by reading God's Word. You may isolate the servant of God in a dungeon, but give him a Bible and a candle and he can still tell you what time it is and what is going on. Indeed, he will need only two small letters written by a weary old preacher in a Roman jail.

Paul's letters to Timothy do not read like the modern success story. Here is no collection of platitudes by a prosperous retired dominie who has feathered his nest, or an ex-prophet promoted into silence, his message hushed by the powers that be. Instead we have the last charge of a grizzled old warrior. Of course those who deny that the Scriptures are God-breathed will dismiss the matter by saying that Paul was only a bilious old bachelor in a depressing dungeon, and since "everything looks yellow to a jaundiced eye," his view of the times was necessarily dismal. But some of us still believe that this holy man spoke as he was moved by the Holy Spirit.

In these letters we have a pattern for the Christian in these last days. Here is a test case. According to the modern pitch, Paul should have written, "Well, Timothy, I used to be dogmatic and exclusive, but I've mellowed (which is often the first stage of spoiling!). I used to preach that there was only one way to be saved, but I've become tolerant in my old age. I see good in all religions. Even paganism is not as bad as I once thought. Then, there are other groups who believe almost as we do. We need them all to swell our numbers and a syncretism (dignified word for "hash") of the good points in all faiths. Our despised little sect will never do the job."

Paul did not mellow into an indiscriminating amiability. He ended as he had started and kept his batting average good to the end of the season. There was only one gospel, and if even an angel preached any other, let him be damned! He did not foresee a converted world; the last days would be perilous. He did not say, "Cheer up, Timothy, the time will come when they will welcome the gospel." Instead, the time would come when they would not endure it.

The very fact that the truth is not popular is all the more reason for preaching it. The very fact that men will not endure it is a reason for seeing that they get it. It is not our responsibility to make it acceptable; it is our duty to make it available.

Paul knew nothing about popular religious diplomacy or summit conferences with unbelievers to work out a compromise. He could have made it easier for himself if he had mixed the gospel with paganism, but he was willing to be the scum of the earth and a spectacle to the world rather than give up the scandal of the cross. He knew that we are saved, not by being religious, but by being righteous, and that the only righteousness God accepts is Jesus Christ made unto us righteousness. That makes it narrow and exclusive and foolishness to this world. Paul knew nothing of a catch-all Christianity, a great common denominator based on the Fatherhood of God and brotherhood of man. He believed that our Lord meant what He said when He declared, "No man cometh unto the Father, but by me" (John 14:6). If we reject that "Gospel of No Other Name," we cannot be Christians, though we be as selfless as Gandhi or as humanitarian as Schweitzer.

I shudder to imagine how many churches would not let Paul into their pulpits today. His world-view would not be acceptable to ecclesiastics out to build a world-church. It is almost impossible for modern religious leaders to gear themselves to Paul's picture of the last days. It does not minister to our religious pride. It does not sound big enough. There is not much room for impressive statistics. It does not fit into the notion that the

Kingdom can be brought in by our efficiency and promotion. It is not popular and we are ashamed of it. We are for cooperating with the world and its religions to work out a program of peace and brotherhood. Paul would have made a poor delegate to that kind of conference.

Then, of course, the church has moved out on the boulevard and all the best people in town belong to it. One hundred million Americans claim church affiliation. The problem used to be that most people did not claim to believe in Christ, but now sinners claim church connections and it is harder than ever to win them to Christ. Plenty of people might be saved if they had not joined a church! They remind us of those in John's Gospel, of whom it is written, "Many believed in his name... *But...*" (2:23-24). There were not many hangers-on in Paul's day. You had to mean business to be a Christian. That was before Constantine made it fashionable to be a church member and filled churches with baptized pagans, a sad procedure prevalent to this day.

We must make up our minds about whether we will accept Paul's world outlook and pay the price of belonging to his despised sect. It will take plenty of grace to resist popular pressure to merge into one agreeable brotherhood bound by some general belief in God. Any man who dares to say a word against it will be called unchristian, for part of the strategy of the mock angel is to put over his delusions in the last days under religious auspices. Any Micaiah who dares to be an odd number when four hundred prophets bid Ahab and Jehoshaphat go up to Ramoth-gilead had better be prepared for a diet of bread and water. He may not be consigned to a jail, but there are other prisons not behind stone walls, and cages not barred with iron.

How are we to conduct ourselves in times like these? Take another look at Paul. Not only did the future of the age look dark, but circumstances were against him. On the human level he had good reason to be discouraged. He was the greatest of all gospel preachers, with all the world around him in need of the gospel—and he was in prison! He could have asked, "Why did this have to happen to me? I am needed in Ephesus and

Philippi and Corinth. I am the Indispensable Man!" Paul was not able to "retire." He had no foundation, no tax-free corporation to support him. He did not even have Social Security! No wealthy friends subsidized him. He wrote to Timothy, "Come before winter" (2 Timothy 4:21). He asked for his old cloak. The damp, dark, dismal dungeon was bad for neuritis, bursitis, arthritis. He must wrap something around his creaking bones.

Then some of his friends had failed him. Demas had forsaken him, having loved this present world. That is always the trouble when Demas forsakes Paul. People who gamble, dance, and frequent the theater have something worse wrong with them; these are but symptoms of a deeper disease. One may allay the symptoms and still have the disease. When we get rid of the disease we remove the symptoms. Yet symptoms are important and are not to be ignored. Do not forget that plenty of people who don't do things we call "worldly" still love the world. Demas does not always smoke or drink or dance; he may be a church deacon, go to Bible conferences, be an ardent fundamentalist theologically, and still love this present world.

Alexander the coppersmith had done Paul much evil. (Some evangelists, noting the pennies in the love offering, still blame the coppersmith for much evil!) But Paul left Alexander in God's hands to reward according to his works. "Say not thou, I will recompense evil; but wait on the Lord, and he shall save thee" (Proverbs 20:22). Paul added this word about Alexander: "Of whom be thou ware also; for he hath greatly withstood our words" (2 Timothy 4:15). Some people will bear watching and some are to be avoided. It doesn't pay to get chummy with Alexander the coppersmith.

Then there was Trophimus whom Paul left lying ill at Miletum. I do not know why he was not healed. Maybe it was chastisement and he had not yet learned his lesson. Maybe he had no faith for healing. Maybe he got better later. I can hear some of the gossip: "Paul may have healed the impotent man at Lystra and the demonized girl in Philippi, but he failed with Trophimus!" Miletum was one spot on Paul's map where the exception did not seem to fit the rest of the program. We all have these breaks in the pattern—the miracle that didn't happen, the loved one not saved, the prayer not answered as we hoped, the thorn in the flesh, the place where we seemed to labor in vain. We have to leave Trophimus sick and allow for Miletum on our itinerary.

But there is the other side: Doctor Luke was faithful; John Mark returned; and there was Timothy. We may have our Demases and Alexanders, but God makes up for them with an Onesimus begotten in our bonds. Let us not spend time checking accounts to see whether we are gaining more Marks than we are losing Demases. Let God keep the books!

Note how triumphantly Paul finishes his "world-view from a prison." He does not say, "Hitherto I have had an awful time," but "Henceforth there awaits me a crown." He ends like the spiritual that begins, "Nobody knows the trouble I see," and finished with "Glory, hallelujah!" One also thinks of the little native girl on a mission field who threw down her heavy load after a long journey and exclaimed, "Hallelujah, I'm tired!"

Paul is not bitter. He does not spend his last days condemning and correcting the brethren. He does not sling mud and thereby lose ground. He does not shovel filth, for the smell rubs off and if we stir garbage we shall be remembered as trash collectors. He ends: "And the Lord shall deliver me from every evil work, and will preserve me unto his heavenly kingdom" (2 Timothy 4:18). In jail, forsaken of friends, he is still not impressed with the grandeur of the Roman Empire but with the final success of the Kingdom of God. He has not the slightest doubt of that. It didn't look like it then. It doesn't look like it now. But above all the tumult our Saviour says, "Fear not, little flock, for it is your Father's good pleasure to give you the Kingdom." Khrushchev may say, "He who laughs last laughs best," but the last laugh will be God's, not Khrushchev's. "He that sitteth in the heavens shall laugh: the Lord shall have them in derision" (Psalm 2:4).

Here is our pattern in times like these: let "The kings of the earth set themselves, and the rulers take counsel together, against the Lord, and against his anointed..." (Psalm 2:2); "... the Lord shall deliver me from every evil work, and will preserve me unto his heavenly kingdom: to whom be glory for ever and ever. Amen" (2 Timothy 4:18).

To obtain additional copies of this book, and to see a list of
other great Christian titles, visit our web site:
www.KingsleyPress.com

Printed in Great Britain
by Amazon